THE ART OF
SHAOLIN
KUNG FU

THE SECRETS OF KUNG FU FOR SELF-DEFENSE HEALTH AND ENLIGHTENMENT

By the same author

The Art of Chi Kung
The Complete Book of Tai Chi Chuan
The Complete Book of Zen
Chi Kung for Health and Vitality

For Mr. Wong's web site, please visit
http://shaolin-wahnam.tripod.com

THE ART OF
SHAOLIN
KUNG
FU

THE SECRETS OF KUNG FU FOR SELF-DEFENSE HEALTH AND ENLIGHTENMENT

FU

WONG KIEW KIT

TUTTLE PUBLISHING
Boston • Rutland, Vermont • Tokyo

First published in the United States and Canada in 2002 by Tuttle Publishing, an imprint of Periplus Editions (HK) Ltd., with editorial offices at 153 Milk Street, Boston, Massachusetts 02109.

Published in 2001 by Vermilion, 20 Vauxhall Bridge Road, London SW1V 2SA

LC Card No. 2002112453

ISBN 0-8048-3439-3

Distributed by:

North America, Latin America &
Europe
Tuttle Publishing
Distribution Center
Airport Industrial Park
364 Innovation Drive
North Clarendon, VT 05759-9436
Tel: (802) 773-8930
Fax: (802) 773-6993

Asia Pacific
Berkeley Books Pte Ltd
130 Joo Seng Road
#06-01/03 Olivine Building
Singapore 368357
Tel: (65) 6280-1330
Fax: (65) 6280-6290

Japan & Korea
Tuttle Publishing
Yaekari Bldg., 3F
5-4-12 Ōsaki, Shinagawa-ku
Tokyo 141 0032
Tel: (03) 5437-0171
Fax: (03) 5437-0755

First edition
06 05 04 03 02   10 9 8 7 6 5 4 3 2 1

Printed in the United States of America

This book is dedicated to my beloved father Wong York Sang, and my beloved mother Bok Pik Yoke, who are now in the Western Paradise, and whose love and kindness bestowed on me I can never repay.

CONTENTS

LIST OF ILLUSTRATIONS

PREFACE

Shaolin Kung Fu sounds like magic to many people, for they have learned that it is not only an effective martial art and an excellent system for health and vitality, it is also a way to spiritual joy. Those who have the privilege to meet genuine Shaolin masters or to have a more than superficial knowledge of Shaolin tradition will appreciate that this is not an exaggerated claim. Shaolin Kung Fu, together with the related arts of Shaolin Chi Kung and Zen or meditation, was taught in great secrecy in Shaolin Monastery, which is regarded as the 'foremost monastery beneath heaven'.

Shaolin Monastery was the imperial temple situated at the Central Sacred Summit of China, where emperors of every dynasty since its establishment ascended to pray on behalf of the people. Yet the main reason for its prestigious title as 'the foremost monastery beneath heaven' was not this imperial connection, but the marvellous arts taught there. It is no historical coincidence that some of the best generals in Chinese history, like Yuan Zhong of the Tang Dynasty, Yue Fei of the Song Dynasty, and Chi Ji Guang of the Ming Dynasty, had their martial training in the Shaolin tradition.

Although Shaolin Chi Kung is not as well known as Shaolin Kung Fu, probably because it is a more advanced art and was therefore preserved in more secrecy, its contribution to today's needs, especially in managing stress and relieving physical and emotional illness, is even more immediate and necessary. Professor Qian Xue Sen, the father of the Chinese rocket, believed that the greatest medical breakthrough of this century would be made through Chi Kung, the understanding and practice of man's vital energy. It is Shaolin Chi Kung, with its development of internal force that has baffled many martial artists, that enables Shaolin Kung Fu to soar to its heights and reach its depths. This book will provide some useful methods for internal force training.

Probably the most important yet least known Shaolin teaching, however, is on Zen, which is the highest form of Shaolin Kung Fu. Not many people, even among those who practise Zen, are aware that all schools of Zen in the world today originated from Shaolin Monastery. Zen is regarded as the most direct form of spiritual cultivation, where enlightenment is attained in an instant. The hallmark of Zen is experience not speculation or intellectualization; one attains a Zen awakening by direct-ly experiencing it, not by merely understanding its philosophy. This book will show you how to train for a Zen awakening. It is Zen that elevates Shaolin Kung Fu to its position as the greatest martial art in the world. This is a claim which martial artists of other styles, understandably, will vehemently oppose, but which even they may concede after reading this book.

In my many years of teaching the Shaolin arts, people have sought my advice on the following three questions:

- How can Shaolin Kung Fu be applied for self-defence?
- How can internal force be trained?
- How can practising Shaolin Kung Fu enable one to experience spiri-tual joy?

This book aims to answer these and other relevant questions. The histor-ical and philosophical aspects of Shaolin Kung Fu are also explained, as many people, especially from Western societies, have frequently indicated to me their difficulty in obtaining such information, which is necessary for a proper appreciation of Shaolin Kung Fu. Nevertheless, this book is mainly a practical guide.

The large number of people from both the East and the West who practise Kung Fu but do not know its combat application is alarming. It has become normal for many Kung Fu students nowadays to learn only routine sets, which is actually only the first stage of Shaolin Kung Fu training, without ever progressing to more advanced stages. This is unfor-tunate because not only is Shaolin Kung Fu a very effective fighting art, but the invaluable aspects of health and vitality as well as the development of the noble personality for which true Shaolin disciples are noted, are derived from training in Shaolin Kung Fu as a martial art, and not as a demonstrative form to please spectators.

A few of my students have asked me a particularly searching question: Why do so many Kung Fu students, knowing that Kung Fu is a very effective fighting art, apparently do nothing about it when they are not getting any benefit in terms of self-defence? There are various reasons for this, but instead of dwelling on them, a major portion of this book is devoted to providing helpful principles and methods to enable Kung Fu students to train themselves to be competent martial artists using such Shaolin methods as specific techniques, combat sequences, sparring sets, force training, tactics and strategies. It must also be emphasized that the Shaolin teaching is opposed to brutality and aggressiveness; if you are looking for a book to turn you into a street fighter, you have definitely chosen the wrong one.

While combat efficiency is a primary function of Shaolin Kung Fu, a more immediate and useful benefit in our law-abiding society is attaining radiant health and vitality. This can be effectively achieved through Shaolin Chi Kung, which represents an advanced stage of Shaolin Kung Fu training. Chi Kung, the art of developing vital energy, not only enhances one's Kung Fu ability and performance but also promotes emotional and mental development. This book will show you how.

The training of the mind is further enhanced in Zen, or meditation, which will lead Shaolin Kung Fu to the greatest heights and depths. The wisdom of the Shaolin teaching, which reflects the teaching of Buddhism, is awe-inspiring. Since Buddhism is not a religion as the term is usually understood in the West, but a quest for spiritual joy, the Shaolin arts can be practised by people of any race, culture or religion. Throughout Shaolin history, there have been masters who explicitly professed Taoism, Christianity, Islam and other religions. Cosmic truths like the relativity of time and space, multi-dimensional realms of existence, different levels of consciousness, and seas of myriad stars and galaxies have not only been taught but actually perceived by Shaolin masters in their deep meditation centuries before our modern scientists accepted their validity.

The highest attainment of Shaolin Kung Fu is spiritual fulfilment, irrespective of one's religion, and this is sometimes achieved through Shaolin Chi Kung but usually through Zen. The highest spiritual fulfilment is known in the Shaolin teaching as enlightenment, which is a Buddhist term meaning the liberation of the illusory personal self to realize the Supreme Reality, and which has been described by different religious teachers as the return to God, the union with the Ultimate Truth, or the merging with the Cosmos.

This book therefore covers all important aspects of Shaolin Kung Fu, many of which are not readily available to the public in general, and fulfils a most extensive range of needs for the young, the middle-aged and older people. The young, at heart as well as in years, will find the more dynamic aspects of Shaolin Kung Fu fascinating, not only in opening a vista of combative techniques and skills different from those they have been accustomed to, but perhaps more importantly in providing a training programme that gives them vitality, stamina, quick judgement and mental freshness.

The middle-aged, many of whom may have endured chronic illness, stress and psychotic problems, will find the energy flow of Shaolin Kung

Fu rewarding. If they consistently practise the Chi Kung exercises described in this book, they have a good chance of relieving their health problems. Those who are already healthy will find the graceful, internal aspects of Shaolin Kung Fu training enhances their physical, emotional and mental well-being, so that they can get more out of their daily work and play.

Those who are older, not necessarily in age but in their development and aspirations, will find the spiritual aspect of Shaolin Kung Fu exciting, as it answers questions such as 'What is the purpose of life?', 'Where will I ultimately go to?' and 'What actually is cosmic reality?' and provides practical methods for understanding them. They will appreciate the Zen tenet of experiencing truth directly, and not merely intellectualizing possibilities.

Those who are used to thinking of Shaolin Kung Fu as nothing more than a fighting art will probably find the claims in this book unbelievable. Genuine Shaolin Kung Fu, especially at the advanced levels of Chi Kung and Zen, was taught to very special people, such as emperors, generals and selected disciples. A basic tenet of the Shaolin teaching, which is an echo of the Buddha's advice to his followers, is that one should not accept anything on faith alone, nor on the reputation of the masters, but practise the arts diligently for a reasonable length of time, and then assess the results according to one's understanding and experience.

In conclusion I wish to thank Ms Julia McCutchen, the Editorial Director, and her capable team at Element Books for their patience and understanding; Ms Doreen Montgomery of Rupert Crew, my literary agent, for her invaluable assistance; and my senior disciples, Shaolin Master Cheong Huat Seng and Shaolin Master Goh Kok Hin for respectively taking the photographs and posing as my 'opponent' for the illustrations in this book.

Wong Kiew Kit
Grandmaster
Shaolin Wahnam Kung Fu and Chi Kung

1

WHAT IS KUNG FU?

Don't Waste Your Time Over Flowery Fists

❖ *Great Kung Fu like Shaolin and Taijiquan is not just a martial art.*

Four Aspects of Kung Fu

Have you ever been threatened by someone out to take your life or rob you? Probably not, for ours is a law-abiding society. But still there is a possibility, no matter how remote, that it could happen, and even if it is just as a protection against this possibility, it is worth practising Kung Fu. There are other, even better, reasons, and we shall discuss them later in this chapter. But first we need to understand what Kung Fu is.

It may seem surprising, but many people who practise Kung Fu do not actually know its true meaning. Some equate learning Kung Fu patterns with practising Kung Fu; others maintain that they practise Kung Fu for health and not for fighting. Many people have spent years learning Kung Fu without understanding its depth and dimension, and without any clear objectives in their training. Needless to say, they have wasted much of their time, despite their devotion to the art.

What then is Kung Fu? Briefly, it is a classical Chinese martial art, practised today by people of different races, cultures and religions. But although this definition is true, it is inadequate to show Kung Fu's extensive scope and the tremendous benefits its practice can bring. We shall have a better understanding if we discuss what constitutes Kung Fu.

All styles of Kung Fu can be divided into four aspects or dimensions:

- form
- force or skill
- application
- philosophy

The Visible Aspect of Form

Kung Fu form is its visible aspect. Because it is the part that we can easily see, form is often mistaken by many people for the *whole* of Kung Fu.
Poetically, Kung Fu masters refer to form as the 'body' of Kung Fu.

The two most obvious manifestations of Kung Fu form are patterns
and sets. A pattern refers to a particular way in which a practitioner holds
the hands, legs and body in position or motion. Sometimes it may refer
to a short series of actions. For example, a practitioner may spread out
both arms, stand upright on one leg, and kick out the instep of the other
leg. This action is a pattern, and is known in Shaolin Kung Fu as White
Crane Flaps its Wings.

A set is formed when numerous patterns are linked together for the
convenience of training. Some sets are short, consisting of about 36 patterns; some are intermediate, with about 72 patterns; others are long, with
about 108 patterns. These numbers are only guidelines, and are generally
applicable to Shaolin Kung Fu. In Taiji Kung Fu or Taijiquan, the popular simplified Taiji set composed by a council of Taijiquan masters in
China to meet modern demand, consists of 24 patterns, while the orthodox Chen style Taijiquan set consists of 83 patterns and the long set in
Yang style Taijiquan consists of 108 patterns. (Taijiquan is pronounced and
often spelt 'T'ai Chi Ch'uan'.)

The patterns are chosen and arranged to form a set for one or more
of the following reasons:

For easy remembering. This is the basic reason why Kung Fu patterns
are arranged into sets rather than practised individually as in some martial
systems like Western boxing and judo. In some sets of this type, all the patterns are different from one another, and the set is generally short. The
Kung Fu set illustrated in Chapter 9, Shaolin Five Animals, belongs to this
type.

For combat application. Certain patterns are particularly useful for
certain combat situations. Moreover, for technical reasons certain arrangements of pattern sequences are favourable. Patterns are therefore linked
according to these two principles to help students learn combat application. The famous Shaolin set Taming a Tiger is a good example.

For force training. Uninformed students may sometimes wonder why
some patterns which have no apparent combat functions are included in
a Kung Fu set. The answer is often that they are meant for force training.
The Iron Wire set of Southern Shaolin is a classic example.

For special skills. Kung Fu masters usually specialize in some chosen skills, like Iron Palm, No-Shadow Kicks and Holds and Grips. The patterns of some sets are arranged so that these skills can be used to the best advantage. An example is the Five Monkeys set, which specializes in agility.

The ways in which patterns may be organised into sets are classified like this purely for the convenience of study, however. Although the construction of sets is usually based on one of the above four principles, most also include the other principles in varying degrees. For example, while Taming a Tiger is constructed principally with combat application in mind, it also includes a few patterns for force training at the beginning.

The Importance of Force Training

If you learn only Kung Fu form but never develop Kung Fu force, your Kung Fu will be futile even if you study for the rest of your life. Many people have heard this advice, but few really understand its significance, and fewer still put it into practice. Failure to appreciate this advice is probably the single most important reason why of the thousands of students who practise Kung Fu, some for years, only a handful reach a master's level. If you understand and put this invaluable point into practice, you are well on the way to becoming a master.

Force, here, is a poor translation of the Chinese term *gong* (pronounced as 'kung'). Force may be classified as basic or specialized. Basic force refers to a force or skill that can be applied generally, and is transferable from one part of the body to another. Having a solid horse stance, for example, is a form of basic force; it provides a strong, stable foundation, no matter what patterns you may be executing. You can also transfer the basic force of your solid horse stance to your legs to inflict powerful kicks.

Specialized force refers to a force or skill that is localized at a certain part of the body, and is usually limited to a particular application. An example is Iron Palm, which is localized at the palms and limited to palm strikes. This specialized force cannot be transferred to the head or legs, nor does an exponent with Iron Palm necessarily have speed or stamina.

It is useful to have a clear understanding of the difference between force and technique, or *gong* and *fa* in Chinese. Technique refers to methods or ways of attack and defence. It has form and is visible. For example, if you put your leg behind your opponent's leg and push to make him or her fall backward, you demonstrate a technique. But whether you succeed in felling the opponent depends not so much on your technique (unless he or she is incompetent) but on your force or skill. Force or skill refers to your ability and efficiency in using technique. It is formless, invisible and involves accuracy, power and speed.

Force and technique are complementary: we need technique to apply our force, and force to back up our technique. Nevertheless, in advanced Kung Fu it is force rather than technique that constitutes the winning factor in combat. A master is measured by his command of force, not by his knowledge of technique.

Application for Combat and Daily Living

The third aspect of Kung Fu is application. One who practises Kung Fu – any form of Kung Fu – must be able to apply it in combat as well as in his daily life. There are some students who have practised so-called Kung Fu for many years, yet they cannot fight at all, even when it is necessary. What they have practised is not genuine Kung Fu but a demonstrative form referred to by masters as 'flowery fists and embroidery kicks'.

Kung Fu, including Taijiquan, becomes meaningless as a martial art if it is devoid of its fighting function. This of course does not imply that a Kung Fu student must fight to justify the art, or that a Kung Fu exponent is necessarily a better fighter than a practitioner of another martial system, but it is imperative that one who has practised Kung Fu for some time must be able to put up a decent defence when attacked.

Perhaps more important than combat is the peaceful application of Kung Fu in our daily life. A Kung Fu practitioner, for example, should exhibit more zest and vitality in both work and play than an ordinary person, and have calmness of mind and clarity of thought even under demanding situations. If you do not have the strength to run up a flight of stairs despite many years of Kung Fu practice, or if you are easily irritated or nervous, then your Kung Fu practice has been futile. Probably you have not spent time developing Kung Fu force.

Kung Fu Philosophy for Deeper Understanding

Throughout the ages, Kung Fu masters have built up a rich and vast store of philosophy. An understanding of this philosophy constitutes the fourth aspect of Kung Fu. An exponent can still be proficient in Kung Fu without any philosophical knowledge, but such a person would have missed the advantage of learning from the accumulated wisdom of great Kung Fu masters. On the other hand, knowing Kung Fu philosophy alone cannot make a good Kung Fu exponent. It is a practical art; its philosophy can provide excellent guidance, but the exponent must put in a lot of practice to achieve proficiency.

Kung Fu philosophy can help you in at least the following four ways:

- It provides a background understanding of what you are doing so that your training has depth and perspective.
- It saves time by providing you with tested methods that past masters took years to develop, and advising you against pitfalls that you should avoid.
- It summarizes the vast, rich experience and achievements of great masters, often in beautiful, poetic language.
- It expands the mind to vistas of wisdom that you may not even have dreamed of, and if you are ready it inspires you to spiritual fulfilment, the greatest achievement anyone can ever attain.

Great Kung Fu styles like Shaolin and Taijiquan are much more than mere fighting arts. In contrast to some martial arts where the main aim is to win, often brutally, in a boxing ring, or where the practitioners draw inspiration from classical samurais whose mission was to kill indiscriminately as their lords decreed, Shaolin Kung Fu and Taijiquan were developed by and derive their inspiration from Buddhist monks whose hallmark is compassion, and Taoist priests whose preoccupation is to preserve life.

It is significant that the original aim of these arts as set by Bodhidharma and Zhang San Feng, the first patriarchs of Shaolin Kung Fu and Taijiquan respectively, was spiritual development, irrespective of the practitioners' religious conviction or lack of it. If your objectives in practising these arts are not spiritual, an appreciation of their sacred origins, as well as other aspects of their philosophy, will provide you with a wider perspective and understanding of the benefits you can derive from your training.

The Benefits of Kung Fu

Why do many people practise Kung Fu for years yet obtain little benefit, while others make tremendous progress within a comparatively short time? One important reason, among others, is that many people practise aimlessly, whereas the fast students are clear about the benefits they are aiming for.

The benefits of all styles of Kung Fu may be classified into three groups:

- self-defence
- health and fitness
- character training

For great Kung Fu like Shaolin and Taijiquan, we can add another two:

- mind expansion
- spiritual development

These benefits also indicate our purpose in practising Kung Fu. In other words, in discussing the benefits, we will also establish the aims we can set ourselves in our training.

Self-defence is the fundamental aim of Kung Fu. Kung Fu training without its combative dimension is Kung Fu without its essence; it ceases to be Kung Fu, and at best becomes a system of physical exercise.

Some instructors and students claim that their Kung Fu training is only for health, and strictly not for fighting. This is acceptable if they have legitimate reasons, such as wishing to avoid possible challenges or applying Kung Fu techniques to cure some particular illness; but they must still understand that Kung Fu can be used for fighting. If they believe that it is *not* for fighting, then something is seriously wrong; they have forgotten that the term *kung fu means* martial arts.

Of course emphasizing the martial aspect of Kung Fu does not necessarily mean encouraging practitioners to fight. Indeed, true Kung Fu teaching always instructs students to be tolerant and avoid fighting as far as possible. But the ability to defend ourselves and our loved ones should the need arise is a valuable asset. It is only when we know with confidence that we can always defend ourselves effectively that we dare to rise to any occasion, and to right wrongs. In modern society, this psychological need is perhaps more important and more immediate than the physical need actually to fight.

The second great benefit of practising Kung Fu is health and fitness. By health, I do not mean merely being free from illness; I mean an ability to eat with relish, to sleep soundly, to work energetically, to think clearly, and to be calm yet alert. By fitness, I do not mean just the brute strength to do heavy work; I mean the ability to run and jump, to withstand heat, cold or wind in the open, to react speedily, to endure hard work, and to concentrate for some time without feeling mental fatigue.

These qualities of health and fitness will be derived from Kung Fu if we practise it as a martial art. If we ignore the martial aspect and practise it as we would other forms of physical exercise, we will still be healthy but we will miss the opportunity to acquire the type of radiant health and fitness required of top-class martial artists. A Kung Fu expert, for example, is trained to have the stamina to fight for hours, to be forceful enough to strike down a huge opponent who may tower above him or her, and to be calm even when facing a situation of life and death. This will give you an idea of the type of health and fitness you can gain from the martial training of Kung Fu.

Kung Fu is better than other forms of exercise in promoting health and fitness. In swimming, jogging and karate, for example, the fitness acquired diminishes as one grows old, but in Kung Fu it is actually enhanced. This is because Kung Fu is more than physical exercise; it involves Chi Kung and meditation to develop the inner faculties of essence, vital energy and mind.

The third benefit of Kung Fu is character training, which is achieved both extrinsically and intrinsically. Extrinsically, Kung Fu teaching emphasizes moral development as well as physical training, stressing values like respect for the master, righteousness, courage, tolerance and reverence for life.

Intrinsically, the very nature of Kung Fu training is a long process of character building. Wholesome qualities like endurance, perseverance, discipline, loyalty and a calm disposition are prerequisites for progress, especially at higher levels. For example, training in the Horseriding Stance calls for endurance, perfecting some Kung Fu techniques calls for perseverance, unfailing practice in rain or shine calls for discipline. Because of factors like tradition, comradeship and gratitude for the chance to learn a priceless art, good Kung Fu students develop loyalty to their master and fellow classmates. In sparring practice as well as in actual combat, a calm disposition is essential in order to achieve an accurate judgement of an opponent's movement. All these qualities, acquired through Kung Fu training, are of course transferable to daily life.

Mind Expansion and Spiritual Development

Great Kung Fu like Shaolin and Taijiquan is not just a martial art. Taijiquan was first developed at the Purple Summit Temple on Wudang Mountain, one of the most sacred centres of Taoism, by Taoist priests who had dedicated their lives to the quest for longevity and immortality. At its advanced level, the study of Taijiquan expands the mind to investigate the secrets of the Cosmos. Taijiquan philosophy opens the practitioner's mind to the Taoist teaching on the mysteries of man and the universe, described by such concepts as yin-yang, *wu-xing* or the five elemental processes, and *bagua* or the eight trigrams.

The highest stage of Taijiquan training is *jing-zuo* or silent sitting, which means meditation. While *jing-zuo* can enhance the martial as well as the health aspect of Taijiquan, its primary aim is spiritual cultivation. The supreme objective is nothing short of the Taoist attainment of unity with the Cosmos.[1]

Shaolin Kung Fu, on the other hand, was developed in the famous Shaolin Monastery, which was no ordinary monastery; it was an imperial temple where emperors of every dynasty ascended to pray on behalf of the people. Hence, Shaolin monks were no ordinary monks; they included some of the best generals, ministers, poets, philosophers and other great minds of the empire. Many princes renounced their luxurious palace lives to pursue higher development at the Shaolin Monastery. It is no surprise, therefore, that the Shaolin Monastery was both a collecting and a diffusing centre for some of the best teachings of the Chinese civilization.

As the foremost Buddhist monastery in China, Shaolin Monastery naturally inherited the rich legacy of the Buddha's teaching. And if you think that the Buddha's teaching was only about religious topics, think again. Centuries before modern scientists, the Buddha and other masters explained reality in terms of subatomic particles and energy (called *dharmas* and *kriya* in Buddhism), the relativity of time and space (*patiyasamutpada*), different levels of consciousness (*vijnana*), multi-dimensional existence (*triloka*), the illusion of the external world (*maya*) and millions of worlds as specks of dust in cosmic cycles (*kalpas*).

The mind expansion of Shaolin masters in the understanding of such awe-inspiring wisdom is not merely intellectual, but more importantly experiential. In other words, Shaolin masters do not just read about such wisdom in sutras or Buddhist scriptures, but directly experience these different levels of reality in their meditation. After all, Zen, which is the highest of the Shaolin arts, is the training of the mind.

Shaolin Kung Fu at the highest level leads to Zen. Many people may be unaware that Zen, or *Chan* as it is known in Chinese, was first developed at the Shaolin Monastery, blossomed in China during the Tang and Song dynasties, and later spread to Japan and other countries. The supreme aim of Zen in Shaolin Kung Fu, just as the supreme aim of *jing-*

zuo or Silent Sitting in Taijiquan, is spiritual fulfilment, the highest accomplishment any person can ever attain.

Although not all people who practise Kung Fu are ready for or interested in spiritual development, an understanding of its scope and depth, especially the greatest Kung Fu like Shaolin and Taijiquan, will add a new dimension and meaning to your practice, making you aware that the potential benefits of your training go far beyond self-defence and keeping fit. This is a practical book, however. You will acquaint yourself with the combative and health aspects of Shaolin Kung Fu before venturing into the mind and spirit. But first you need a clear understanding of the historical background and various styles of Kung Fu, so that when you meet terms like *wushu* and *quanfa* or famous styles like Bagua Palm and Praying Mantis Kung Fu, you will know what they mean and how they fit into the matrix of fundamental Kung Fu knowledge.

<u>2</u>

THE HISTORICAL DEVELOPMENT OF CHINESE MARTIAL ARTS

The Changing Concept and Content of Kung Fu

❖ *Chinese martial arts have been known by over 40 different terms!*

Do you know why you will not find the term *kung fu* in classical Chinese texts, although there is a lot of Kung Fu material recorded in history and literature? Did you know that boxing and wrestling were popular sports in China centuries ago? A brief history of Kung Fu from the Stone Age to the modern day will help to clarify the way in which the art has developed in its present form.

The concept as well as the content of Kung Fu varies according to the needs and fashion of a particular time. For example, during the time of the Zhou Dynasty (*c*1030–480 BCE), archery and horseriding were prominent aspects of Kung Fu, or *jiji* as it was generally known then. Today, we normally think of it as involving unarmed combat patterns and prearranged sparring.

In this chapter we shall look at the extensive and comprehensive concept and content of Chinese martial arts from earliest times. In the next two we shall examine the development of the various schools of Kung Fu as we generally know it today.

Kung Fu in Prehistoric and Ancient Times

Kung Fu is older than civilization. As long as there have been people on earth, there has been fighting. And as long as there has been fighting, people have devised ways of helping themselves fight well. These developed into an art, which was Kung Fu, and it occurred before people began farming and settlement, which were the beginnings of civilization.

In the past, Kung Fu was known by other names. In fact throughout history (and prehistory), Chinese martial arts have been known by over 40 different terms! Certain names were popular at certain periods. The term 'Kung Fu' is comparatively modern – it has been used only in the 20th century. Hence, if you examine classical Chinese texts, you will not find the term *kung fu* used. The term *wushu*, which has been popular since 1949 was also used from the 3rd to the 6th century CE. The term that was most commonly used from the 3rd century BCE to the 19th century CE is *wuyi*. *Wu* means martial, and *yi* means art. Both *wushu* and *wuyi* are translated as 'martial art', but semantically, *yi* is the more precise in its meaning.

Other common terms used to refer to Chinese martial arts in the past are listed below, with their literal English translations.

jueli	combating strength
juedi	wrestling
jiji	techniques of fighting
wuji	martial techniques
xiangpu	butting combat
xiangpo	inter–combat
shoupo	hand combat or boxing
zuojiao	gripping and throwing
quanfa	fist techniques
quanshu	art of the fist

Chinese archaeological discoveries show that the Stone-Age Chinese were well versed in martial arts and had large quantities of axes, spears and swords made from stones and bones. The earliest of these weapons, dated to more than 7,000 years ago, were of a surprisingly high standard. These prehistoric men employed martial arts individually in fighting amongst themselves and against animals, as well as collectively in tribal wars. Archaeological evidence suggests that during periods of peace, they performed dances based on martial art movements. Hence, the dance-like sets that you perform now when you practise Kung Fu may be traced back to these prehistoric ancestors!

During the metal age in the Hsia and Shang Dynasties (*c*2000–1030 BCE), weapons were made from copper and later bronze. The earliest Chinese writings on bones and tortoise shells depicted many martial art concepts. By the time of the Zhou Dynasty (*c*1030–480 BCE), Chinese martial arts, known as *quanyong* (fist fighting), and *shoupo* (hand combat) at that time, had developed into sophisticated systems with profound philosophies. The principles of yin-yang, *wu-xing* (the five elemental processes), and *bagua* (or *pakua*, the eight archetypal symbols) were employed to explain many martial art concepts.

During the Warring States period (480–221 BCE) various governments as well as the general public placed tremendous importance on martial arts, which were known as *jiji* (techniques of fighting) and *xiangpo* (inter-combat) at that time. Archery and horseback fighting became essential aspects of martial arts. The world-famous classic on warfare, *The Military Strategies of Sun Tzu*, was written in this period.

After Shi Hwang Ti had unified China and established the Qin Dynasty (221–207 BCE), he introduced the sports of *shoupo* (boxing) and *juedi* (wrestling), where two contestants fought each other in an enclosure. These were probably the earliest boxing and wrestling matches in the world.

The Glorious Han and Tang

The term *wuyi* first appeared in the Han Dynasty (207 BCE–220 CE) and has remained the most popular term for martial arts among the Chinese throughout the ages. At this time it included archery, horseback fighting, weightlifting, boxing, wrestling, unarmed combat, fighting with weapons, set practice and sparring.

The sports of boxing and wrestling remained very popular, especially with the encouragement of Han Wu Ti, the emperor who was well known for the Han military expansion. Han records showed that contesting boxers were bare to the waist and wore shorts just like our modern boxers, but they did not wear gloves and were not restricted by safety rules. Wrestling matches were safer; the contestants were not allowed to hit or kick, and they won by points gathered from throwing opponents to the ground.

Swordsmanship became very popular and highly respected. Not only warriors but also scholars were engaged in sword practice, and some even carried swords for personal adornment. Sword-fighting techniques were linked together to form routine sets, which were often performed as dances, frequently by pretty maidens who were not trained in martial arts; hence they sometimes degenerated into merely demonstrative forms. However, sword duels were common between martial art experts to settle disputes.

After the fall of the Han Dynasty, China broke up into numerous contesting states for about 400 years. This period is often conveniently called

The Two Chin and North-South Dynasties (221–617 CE). During this time, patterns using various weapons as well as unarmed fighting patterns were linked together to form routine sets. The original purpose was to enable martial artists to remember the patterns better. In this way routine sets were established in Chinese martial arts. These sets, sometimes performed for demonstrations, were quite different from individual techniques, which were primarily practised for fighting. There was also a difference in martial art training between routine set practice and sparring.

It was during this time that the Venerable Bodhidharma came from India to China to spread Buddhism. In 527 CE he settled down in the Shaolin Monastery in Henan Province, and inspired the development of Shaolin Kung Fu. This marked a watershed in the history of Kung Fu, because it led to a change of course, as Kung Fu became institutionalized. Before this, martial arts were known only in a general sense. It was only after the inception of Shaolin Kung Fu that names were used to label the various schools, like Taijiquan, Bagua, Wing Choon, Eagle Claw, Praying Mantis and so on. Indeed, Kung Fu, as we understand it today, started from Shaolin.

The historical development of the various styles will be described in the next chapter; let us now return to the mainstream of Chinese martial arts.

China was unified again under the Tang Dynasty (618–906 CE). The Imperial Martial Examination to select outstanding warriors for the state was introduced during the reign of Empress Wu. This examination, like the corresponding Imperial Civil Examination to select scholars to fill high civil posts, was comprehensive and elaborate, graduating from district and provincial to national level, and held at regular intervals. The examination subjects included horseback fighting, ground fighting, spear techniques, use of various weapons, archery on horseback and on the ground, weightlifting and military strategies.

The sports of boxing and wrestling continued to be widely enjoyed by the public. A different type of wrestling, known as *xiangpu* (butting combat) or *jueli* (combating strength), developed. The contestants wore nothing except a tight loincloth and a hairband. As they could not grasp their opponents' collars or sleeves to effect a throw, their main tactics were butting and pushing them over by their sheer mass. The famous sumo wrestlers of Japan could trace the origin of their art to the *xiangpu* or *jueli* of the Tang Dynasty.

The Song, the Yuan and the Ming

Kung Fu, known at the time as *wuyi* (martial arts) and *wuji* (martial techniques), was exceedingly popular during the Song Dynasty (960–1279 CE). The dynasty's founding emperor himself was a Shaolin Kung Fu expert who initiated the Taiju style.

The Song government strongly encouraged the people to practise *wuyi*, and established martial arts schools and colleges. In 1044 it published the *Grand Classic of Martial Arts*, which included military organization and practice, arts of infantry and cavalry, military movements and camping, strategies and tactics, the manufacture and use of weapons, military geography, and case histories of all important battles before the Song.

Martial arts clubs were popular, and included archers' clubs, lancers' clubs and wrestling clubs. Song documents show that in 1125, for example, there were more than 580 archers' clubs with 240,000 civilian archers in the empire![1] Many *wuyi* experts made a living by public demonstrations of their arts, as travelling showmen or in permanent arenas. Their shows included wrestling, boxing, acrobatics, demonstrations of martial arts sets, weapons, archery and weightlifting. An interesting feature was that many of these experts were women. There were enough of them to justify a new term to describe them – *nu zhan*.

However, during the Yuan Dynasty (1260–1368 CE), when the Mongols ruled China, the Chinese were forbidden to keep weapons or practise martial arts. Nevertheless, the sport of *zuojiao* (gripping and throwing or Mongolian wrestling) was widespread, and some martial artists also practised their arts secretly. Many concealed *wuyi* in the acrobatics and actions of the dramas which were very popular at this time. But although many fighting techniques were preserved in this way, it also quickened the degradation of martial arts into purely demonstrative forms.

The Ming Dynasty (1368–1644 CE) represented a significant landmark in the development of Chinese martial arts, generally known as *wuyi* or *quanfa* (fist techniques) in this period, in that the difference between the martial and the demonstrative aspects became more distinct. On the one hand, many Ming generals employed it as an essential and highly respected part of military training, with regular competitions amongst the soldiers. On the other hand, professional *wuyi* display artists regarded it as a performing art, often adulterating it with flowery movements to please the spectators. The term 'flowery fists and embroidery kicks' was commonly used to describe this type of decorative movement, which gradually became ineffective for combat purposes.

The Ming period also witnessed the establishment of many Kung Fu styles. The Taiju style founded by the first Song emperor, and the Eagle Claw style founded by the famous Song general Yue Fei, both of whom were Shaolin masters, evolved into distinctive schools of Kung Fu. Both arts were initially practised in the armies but later diffused into public practise. The Praying Mantis style was founded in this period by a Shaolin master, Wang Lang.

The distinction between the 'external' and 'internal' schools of Kung Fu was first mentioned in the Ming period. In the much quoted *Elegy of Wang Zhong Nan*, Huang Zhong Yi said that:

> Shaolin Kung Fu is the most famous beneath heaven, and is primarily used for fighting, hence it is external; whereas internal Kung Fu emphasizes the quiescence against the moving, and originated with the Taoist priest Zhang San Feng of the Song period.

In his *Internal Kung Fu*, the famous master of the internal school, Zhang Song Xi, said:

> There are two schools of Kung Fu, namely external and internal. The best known of the external is Shaolin, which is meant mainly for attack. The internal is meant mainly for defence, and is soft.

Many important martial arts classics were written during the Ming period. Some of the greatest works, which are still used as authoritative references today, are *Collections from the Hall of Righteousness* by Yu Da Yau, *New Book of Discipline* by Chi Ji Guang, *Records of Military Formations* by He Liang Chen and *Classic of Martial Matters* by Mao Yuan Yi. All the above writers were great generals who were also Kung Fu masters. These books, which describe not only various types of contemporary Kung Fu but also important matters of warfare, are a reflection of the intimate relationship between martial arts and military affairs at that time.

It was during the Ming period that the spread of Chinese martial arts to Japan was most significant. For example, in 1619 a Kung Fu master, Chen Yuan Bin, arrived in Japan to teach Shaolin Kung Fu, laying the foundation for jujitsu, the forerunner of judo.

The Modern Period

When the Manchus established the Qing Dynasty (1644–1911), the government encouraged *wuyi* in the army, but discouraged it amongst civilians. Many Manchurian generals and administrators were great Kung Fu masters.

The public maintained the practice of martial arts in private schools and clubs. Hence features like individual fighting, unarmed combat, set practice for health and demonstration were emphasized. Other aspects connected with extensive warfare, like military strategies and formations, archery and horseback fighting were neglected. This gradual evolution resulted in the concept and content of Kung Fu that we are familiar with today.

The Qing period was important for the development of the internal styles of Kung Fu. Taijiquan, which had earlier evolved from Shaolin Kung Fu, became widely practised in northern China during this period. The other two major styles of internal Kung Fu, Bagua (Pakua) and Xing Yi, were established. Many imperial guards of the palace practised Bagua Kung Fu.

In southern China, Shaolin Kung Fu prevailed. The Southern Shaolin Monastery in Fujian Province became a rallying centre for revolutionaries aiming to overthrow the Manchurian government. The Manchurian armies razed the monastery and Shaolin masters were dispersed to Guangdong Province, Hong Kong, South-East Asia and America. One of these masters was the Shaolin monk Jiang Nan, who transmitted the Shaolin arts to Yang Fa Kun. Yang Fa Kun transmitted the arts to Ho Fatt Nam, my master, who kindly and generously taught them to me.

Dr Sun Yat Sen's successful revolution in 1911 brought the long dynastic history of China to a close. Many of the revolutionaries were secular Shaolin disciples. Numerous martial arts organizations were formed, the most important being Jing Wu (Ching Woo) Athletic Association, which was founded by a Kung Fu expert, Huo Yuan Jia, and had branches in many parts of China and South-east Asia. In 1926 the Kuomintang government changed the term *wushu*, which was commonly used then, to *guoshu*, meaning 'national art'.

Ironically, the standard of *guoshu* deteriorated further into flowery forms for demonstration during this period. Two reasons for this were that the emergence of firearms greatly reduced the importance of martial arts training in the army, and that the Kuomintang government only paid lip service to the promotion of *guoshu*. For instance, the Kuomintang army in Taiwan today is trained in taekwondo instead of in *guoshu*, their national art!

In contrast, the Communist government which replaced the Kuomintang in China has done a great deal to revive the glory and greatness of Chinese martial arts, which they renamed *wushu*. There are working committees at national, provincial and district levels to study and promote the arts; specialized *wushu* schools and colleges have been established; *wushu* teams are sent overseas for promotional demonstrations; numerous books giving invaluable information on *wushu* have been published; and national and international *wushu* tournaments are held. *Wushu* is already included in the Asian Games, and is expected be included in the next Olympic Games. But to me, the most important contribution of the present Chinese government to *wushu*, and one which may turn out to have the most far reaching consequences, is the restoration of the sacred temple of Kung Fu, the fabulous Shaolin Monastery, which spells magic to many martial arts enthusiasts throughout the world.

3

FROM SHAOLIN TO TAIJIQUAN

Understanding Different Styles of Kung Fu

❖ *The term Kung Fu, which is probably most widely used in English today when referring to Chinese martial arts, is actually very recent, and became popular only in the 20th century.*

There are so many styles of Kung Fu that the uninitiated often become confused. For example, could you tell the difference between, the Long Fist and the Monkey style, or the various types of Taijiquan? And do you know why Chaquan is called the Kung Fu of Muslims?

You will be able to answer these questions by the time you have read this chapter. You will also learn about the historical background to the various styles, their philosophies, important features, and typical forms.

Kung Fu and Quanshu

The term Kung Fu, which is probably most widely used in English today when referring to Chinese martial arts, is actually very recent, and became popular only in the 20th century. It is interesting to note that even now it is seldom used in the Chinese language, except colloquially in the Cantonese dialect. The popular Chinese term, in both Mandarin and Cantonese, and in both the written and the spoken form, which comes closest to the concept of Kung Fu as it is commonly understood by Western users, is *quanshu* or *quanfa*. (the 'q' being pronounced 'ch').

Quanshu means the art of the fist, *quanfa*, the techniques of the fist. If you recall the history of Chinese martial arts as described in the previous chapter, you will remember that *quanshu* and *quanfa* particularly refer to that aspect of Chinese martial arts where unarmed combat in the form of hitting and kicking is emphasized, as opposed to *jueli* or *zuojiao*, for example, where wrestling and throwing respectively are prominent. The terms *quanshu* and *quanfa* also suggest some conceptual difference from the more holistic and inclusive term *wuyi*, which in earlier times included archery and horseriding.

In Chinese, Shaolin Kung Fu is referred to as *Shaolinquan*; Bagua Kung Fu as *Baguaquan*; Praying Mantis Kung Fu as *Tanglangquan*, and so on. *Quan*, which literally means 'fist', is the short form of *quanshu* or *quanfa*, and refers not just to the use of the fist, but to the whole system of Kung Fu, including the use of weapons and methods of force training.

All the various styles of Kung Fu came after Shaolin, and almost all – if not actually all – developed from Shaolin Kung Fu.

Shaolin Kung Fu

The famous Shaolin Monastery, was founded by the Indian Buddhist monk, Batuo, in 495 CE, under the imperial patronage of Emperor Xiao Wen Di of the Northern Wei Dynasty. In 527 CE Bodhidharma, an Indian prince who renounced his luxurious life to become a Buddhist monk, arrived there to teach Buddhism. As he found the monks too weak to practise meditation, the essential way to enlightenment, he taught them a series of external exercises known as the Eighteen Lohan Hands, and a system of internal exercise known as the Classic of Sinew Metamorphosis.

Shaolin was no ordinary monastery. It was the practice of Chinese emperors throughout history to pray to heaven once a year for the peace and prosperity of the people, and they performed the rites at one of the five sacred mountains of China. The Song Mountain where Shaolin Monastery is situated was the Central Sacred Mountain. Hence Shaolin was often visited by emperors and great generals. Some of the generals retired to the monastery to seek spiritual enlightenment. They were martial arts experts, and when they saw the monks practising the Eighteen Lohan Hands, they evolved the physical exercises into Kung Fu movements, which were later known as Shaolin Lohan Kung Fu. They also evolved Sinew Metamorphosis into Shaolin Chi Kung. Chi Kung is the art of developing intrinsic energy.[1]

There are now many different types of Shaolin Kung Fu, each with special features suitable for different people and different needs, but the basic form is Lohan Kung Fu, which is a good style for strong, large exponents, because it uses the advantages of size and strength. Shaolin Chi Kung has also developed into many different types, but Sinew Metamorphosis still remains the fundamental approach to internal force training in Shaolin Kung Fu.

Figures 3.1 and *3.2* show a pattern from Shaolin Lohan Kung Fu and Sinew Metamorphosis respectively.

Fig 3.1 Lohan Emerges from a Cave   **Fig 3.2** Grasping Fists

The conditions at Shaolin Monastery were ideal for Kung Fu training. The environment is among the most scenic in China, and the monks had no worldly problems to distract them. Kung Fu was not just practised as a fighting system, but studied and researched as an art by intelligent, well-disciplined disciples who had a lot of time as well as some of the best masters in the empire to teach them. Their achievements were cumulative, with each generation of masters adding new techniques and skills to a growing repertoire. It is not surprising that soon the monastery became the premier centre for Kung Fu training.

Shaolin Kung Fu was initially taught only to the monks, but later secular disciples were also accepted. After graduation, these secular disciples – and also some monks – spread to various parts of the country to teach the art. Soon the saying, 'Shaolin Kung Fu is the best in the world' was widely accepted. It was later divided into Northern Shaolin and Southern Shaolin.

The volume of the Shaolin arts expanded so much that no one could learn them all in his lifetime and specialization began. The various skills are traditionally known as the Shaolin 72 Arts. These arts are extensive and comprehensive, aiming not only for effective fighting, but also for health, personal growth and enlightenment, and are varied to suit the widely differing needs of the young, the middle aged and the old. Since more arts have been added over the years, the number is actually more than 72. To maintain the tradition there have been minor changes at different periods to the arts that constitute the 72, but the major arts have remained the same. Some examples of these are Iron Palm, Plum Flower Foundation, the Art of Lightness, the Heart Purifying Method and various techniques to enhance different sense organs. The Shaolin 72 Arts are therefore more than just a fighting system.

Changquan or Long Fists

Many styles branched out from the 'parent' Shaolin Kung Fu. The earliest was probably the Taiju style, known in Chinese as *taiju changquan* (meaning the Long Fist style) of the first Song emperor. The term 'long' alludes to the continuous movements of the patterns in their sets, which resemble the continuous flow of the Long River, the name the Chinese give the Yangtze Kiang. Thus, in a performance of Northern Shaolin Kung Fu, individual patterns are not performed in a staccato manner, but in a flowing movement of 10–20 patterns performed without a break like one long continuous wave, followed by another wave of another 10–20 patterns. A set of 60 patterns, for example, is performed with only four or five short pauses, as if it contains only four or five long, continuous patterns. This Taiju style was invented in the 10th century by Zhao Kuang Yin, the founding emperor of the Song Dynasty, who owed much of his empire building to Shaolin Kung Fu.

Later the term Changquan, or Long Fist, began to be used for other styles of Kung Fu where there are fast, forceful, stretching movements and beautiful jumping and kicking techniques, all executed like continuous waves. All Changquan styles are either derived directly from Northern Shaolin or greatly influenced by it. The major styles of Changquan today are Chaquan, Huaquan (Flower Kung Fu), Huaquan (Kung Fu of Essence), Hongquan and Baoquan.

Chaquan, or Cha Kung Fu, was developed by Jamil, a Chinese Muslim living in the later Ming Dynasty. The term is derived from his name: in Chinese, Jamil is pronounced 'Cha-mi-l'. Chaquan is sometimes known as the Kung Fu of Muslims, as it is very popular among the Muslim populations of north-western China. *Figure 3.3* shows a typical pattern from Chaquan.

Chaquan is beautiful to watch and effective for fighting. There are ten parts:

1 Mother and Son
2 Hand Movements
3 Flying Kicks
4 Prosperity and Peace
5 East of the Gate
6 Ambush
7 Plum Flower
8 Continuous Attack
9 Tail Wagging
10 Linked Together

Hongquan (pronounced as 'Hung Ch'uan'), or Hong Kung Fu, is popular in the provinces of Shanxi and Sichuan. It was founded by the famous Shaolin monk Jue Yuan of the Yuan Dynasty, and was named after its two basic sets, Little Hong and Big Hong. It is a popular style of Northern Shaolin Kung Fu.

In Chinese, the word *hong*, meaning 'red', is pronouncd in the same way as another word meaning 'great', which is a fairly common surname. One of the great Southern Shaolin masters was Hong Xi Guan who lived in the Qing Dynasty, and there is a famous style of Southern Shaolin Kung Fu named after him, which is also called Hongquan. Although the two words are written differently in Chinese characters, they are exactly the same when written in Roman script, so we need to be sure which style of Hongquan is referred to. Southern Hongquan will be discussed in the next chapter. *Figure 3.4* shows a typical pattern of Northern Hongquan.

Baoquan, or Cannon Kung Fu, is a very old style. Documents show that the famous Shaolin monk, Yuan Zhong, gave a demonstration of Baoquan in front of the first Tang emperor during his inauguration as a general. It is called Baoquan because it is noted for its speed and power. There are 12 basic techniques in this style, known as the 12 Cannons.

Huaquan, or Flower Kung Fu, was invented by a Shaolin master, Gan Feng Chi, in the Qing Dynasty. *General Discussion on Flower Kung Fu*, the prototype of this style written by the master himself is still available, and has been reprinted. This style of Kung Fu emphasizes fast, short techniques, counter-attacking the opponent with distracting movements. It is useful for small exponents faced with bigger opponents. It stresses short combat sequences for practical fighting rather than long, complete sets for demonstration.

Fig 3.3 A pattern from Chaquan

Figure 3.4 A pattern from Hongquan
(Northern Shaolin)

Fig 3.5 A pattern from Huaquan (Flower Kung Fu)

The Romanized spelling *hua*, meaning 'flower', is pronounced in the first tone. There is another style of Kung Fu, which is also spelt as Huaquan, but with the *hua*, meaning 'beauty' or 'essence', pronounced in the second tone. There is no confusion between these two styles in Chinese because both their written forms and their pronunciations are different; but problems arise when they are written in the Romanized spelling as there is no difference.

Huaquan meaning Kung Fu of Essence combines the essentials of *jing*, *chi* (*qi*)[2] and *shen*, the three fundamental features of Kung Fu, in one unity. *Jing* refers to internal force, *chi* to intrinsic energy, and *shen* to mind power. The basic philosophy of Huaquan rests on the principles of four attacks, eight methods and twelve forms.

The four attacks are hitting, kicking, falling and gripping. The eight methods are hands, eyes, body, footwork, strength, internal force, intrinsic energy and mind power. The 12 forms are moving like waves, being still like mountains, rising like monkeys, lowering like sparrows, standing like cockerels, being stable like pine trees, turning like wheels, stretching like bows, being light like leaves, being heavy like iron, being sharp like eagles, and being fast like wind.

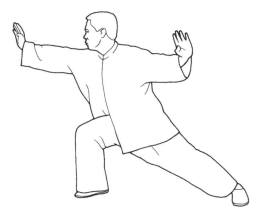

Fig 3.6 A pattern from Huaquan (Kung Fu of Essence)

Yan Qing, Deceptive Movements and the Monkey Style

Yanqingquan, or Yan Qing Kung Fu, was invented by Yan Qing, a Kung Fu master of the Song Dynasty. One day while passing through Shanxi, he met an old priest named Midnight Saint with a well-trained monkey, who addressed Yan Qing as monkey, and his monkey as Yan Qing. The insult led to a quarrel. Midnight Saint told Yan Qing that he should first defeat his monkey before fighting him. But Yan Qing could not even beat the monkey, so he begged Midnight Saint to accept him as a disciple. Thus, Yan Qing Kung Fu is full of deceptive techniques which resemble a monkey's movements.

On another occasion, Yan Qing was being trailed by the police. His footprints in the snow were so deceptive that the police soon lost the trail.

Hence Yan Qing Kung Fu is also called Mi-Zhong-Yi, or the Art of Deceptive Movements. It is popular in the Chinese provinces of Shantung and Shanxi. The great Kung Fu master of the late Qing Dynasty, Huo Yuan Jia, whose Jing Wu (Ching Woo) Athletic Association, helped to spread Kung Fu to many parts of the world, was famous for his Mi-Zhong-Yi.

The Monkey style, or Houquan, was a very old form of Kung Fu. Archaeological findings show that it was already in existence during the Han Dynasty. In his classic *New Book of Discipline* the Ming general Chi Ji Guang mentions it in his discussion of famous contemporary Kung Fu.

The Monkey style is noted for agility, fast attacks and deceptive movements. It is excellent for small exponents; indeed, having a large body is a disadvantage. It exists as a separate school in itself and also as a component of many other schools. My master, Sifu Ho Fatt Nam, is an expert in the Monkey style. An example of the Monkey style Kung Fu pattern is shown in *Figure 3.7*.

Fig 3.7 Listening to the Sound of Zen from Monkey style Kung Fu

The Various Styles of Taijiquan

A very important development took place towards the end of the Song Dynasty. A Taoist master, Zhang San Feng, also spelt as Chang San Foong, retreated to the Wudang Mountain to continue his search for immortality after he had completed his Kung Fu training at Shaolin Monastery. Although the monastery was Buddhist, Shaolin disciples could be of any religion – indeed there were many Taoists, Confucians and people of other religions studying there.

One day Zhang San Feng witnessed a fight between a crane and a snake. This gave him an inspiration that was to have a tremendous effect in the history of Kung Fu. He modified his Shaolin Kung Fu into softer forms, and emphasized *chi* training and meditation. This new type of Kung Fu was known as Wudang 32 Patterns Long Fist. Zhang San Feng is generally credited as the founder of the internal school of Kung Fu.

This Wudang Kung Fu, which is now frequently referred to as Wudang Taijiquan, was passed on to Wang Zhong Yue, and then to Zhang Song Xi. It was then transmitted to Chen Wang Ting, a scholar-general of the late Ming Dynasty, who transformed it into the Taijiquan of Chen Jia Gou village in 18th century, thus, founding Chen style Taijiquan.

At the Chen Jia Gou village, Taijiquan was taught only to members of the Chen family until the time of Chen Chang Xing in the 19th century. Then a young martial arts enthusiast named Yang Lu Chan, who had practised many types of Kung Fu before, was so keen to learn Taijiquan that he gave away his family fortune and worked as a servant for the Chen family. Without anyone knowing, he observed how the members of the family trained, and secretly practised at night, doing this for many years.

One day, the story goes, another master came to the Chen family to challenge, Chen Chang Xing. As he was too old to fight, his eldest son took the challenge, but was badly beaten. The challenger asked for the master, but his disciples tried to prevent Chen Chang Xing's disgrace by telling him that the master was away. The challenger decided to wait, however, and returned every three days to ask for the master. The Chen family had a problem until finally Yang Lu Chan took the challenge and, to everyone's surprise, defeated the challenger, restoring the glory of Taijiquan and the Chen family.

Personally, I find this story unlikely, for two reasons. First a Kung Fu master, especially one who emphasized internal training, would not deteriorate to the point where he could not fight. And secondly, it was not proper for a master, especially the head of a Kung Fu school, to hide behind the pretence that he was not at home when faced with a challenger. The challenger was friendly, not malicious, and it would not be a disgrace to acknowledge the superiority of his Kung Fu.

At that time, to learn Kung Fu secretly behind a master's back was a very grave offence, punishable by death. But, as was to be expected under the circumstances, Chen Chang Xing pardoned Yang Lu Chan, and accepted him as his special disciple.

Yang Lu Chan travelled all over China to meet Kung Fu masters in friendly challenges. Using the Taijiquan that he had learnt from Chen Chang Xing, he always won. Soon he was known as the Invincible Yang.

Later he settled down in Beijing to teach Taijiquan, and he is regarded as the founder of Yang style Taijiquan, although the modification from the Chen to the Yang style was actually done by his grandson Yang Deng Fu. *Figure 3.10* illustrates a pattern from Yang style Taijiquan.

Figure 3.8 Lion Opening Mouth from Wudang Taijiquan

Figure 3.9 Lazily Rolling Up Sleeves from Chen style Taijiquan

Fig 3.10 Low Single Whip from Yang style Taijiquan

After learning from Yang Lu Chan, and then from another Chen master, Chen Jing Ping, Wu Yu Xiang started his own style of Taijiquan, known as Wu style Taijiquan. There is another Wu style Taijiquan, initiated by Wu

Chuan You, who was a disciple of Yang Lu Chan's son, Yang Ban Hou, who in turn also had learned from Wu Yu Xiang. But in Chinese the two 'Wu' are written and pronounced differently.

At the beginning of the 20th century, when he was already 50 years old, Sun Lu Tang, a Kung Fu master who was already accomplished in Bagua and Xingyi Kung Fu, learned Taijiquan from Hao Wei Zhen, the third generation successor of Wu Yu Xiang. Sun Lu Tang combined the arts of Taijiquan, Bagua and Xingyi to found Sun style Taijiquan.

There are therefore numerous styles of Taijiquan. Apart from the traditional Wudang Taijiquan of Zhang San Feng, which is rarely seen now, the oldest style today is Chen style Taijiquan. The most popular, especially outside China, however, is the Yang style. Chen style Taijiquan is comparatively hard and fast, and in many ways resembles Shaolin Kung Fu. Yang style Taijiquan is comparatively slow and soft, and resembles a graceful dance.

Taiji, meaning 'the grand ultimate', refers to the Cosmos. Of all the major styles of Kung Fu, Taijiquan is the most closely related to Taoist philosophy. Its fundamental principle is the concept of yin-yang (*see* page 34), and it is commonly referred to as the soft or internal school. The term 'soft' can be misleading: despite its gentle, graceful appearance, Taijiquan can be very forceful. As the term 'internal' suggests, Taijiquan force is developed mainly by means of the internal training of intrinsic energy and meditation.

Soft and Hard, Internal and External

As we have seen, the various styles of Kung Fu are sometimes classified into the hard or external schools and soft or internal schools. Shaolin Kung Fu and all its derivatives belong to the hard or external schools, whereas Taijiquan, Baguaquan and Xingyiquan belong to the soft or internal schools.

But hard and soft, or external and internal, are arbitary terms. Much of Shaolin Kung Fu, for example, is very soft and internal. In fact there are considerably more soft or internal arts in Shaolin than in Taijiquan. Yet Shaolin is regarded as hard or external, because in a performance it is usually the fast, external movements of the techniques or the hard force, such as in breaking bricks, that impress spectators most. In contrast, a performance of Taijiquan often gives spectators an impression of gentle, graceful movements.

Moreover, in learning Shaolin Kung Fu, one often does a lot of stretching exercises and stance training, which are associated with the hard and external aspects of Kung Fu. On the other hand, a Taijiquan student often starts with flowing movements, which are less vigorous and demanding and are generally associated with the soft aspects. And someone who is lucky enough to have a good Taijiquan master may learn breathing co-ordination and other *chi* training, which are associated with the internal aspects.

Shaolin starts with the hard and external and proceeds to the soft and internal in the advanced stages. Not many people have the patience or the opportunity to reach these advanced stages, so even many Shaolin students mistakenly think that Shaolin Kung Fu is not soft and internal. Some of these soft arts will be described in this book.

Taijiquan starts with the soft and internal, and proceeds to the hard and external in the advanced stages. Advanced Taijiquan students, for example, may hit their bodies forcefully with granules so as to condition themselves to take punches and kicks without sustaining any injury. Such practice is hard. At advanced levels, Taijiquan students engage in fast sparring as training for real fighting. This is external. As only few students reach these advanced levels, many Taijiquan students, especially those who primarily concern themselves only with form practice, mistakenly think that Taijiquan is only soft.

4

A COMPARATIVE STUDY OF KUNG FU

A Pot-Pourri of Bear, Praying Mantis and Crane

❖ *The various ingenious ways masters devised to meet their combat, health and other needs are in themselves fascinating, as well as providing us with suggestions on improving our own art.*

The great military strategist Sun Tzu said that if you understand yourself and understand your opponent you will win a hundred battles out of a hundred. A crucial factor for combat efficiency is to understand the strength and weakness of your opponent's martial art. Understanding the various styles of Kung Fu is excellent for this purpose because virtually all the well-known martial arts techniques in the world are found in Kung Fu. This is not surprising if we remember that Kung Fu has a history many times longer and a volume of practitioners at any one time many times bigger than other martial arts.

Combat efficiency is not the only reason why a comprehensive study of Kung Fu styles should be attempted. The various ways masters devised to meet their combat, health and other needs are in themselves fascinating, as well as providing us with suggestions on improving our own art. For those choosing a martial art to practise, a comparative study is necessary to enable them to make an informed choice, and for those who are already practising a chosen art, such a study may introduce them to techniques and skills not found in their own arts. For Shaolin disciples, it is inspiring to learn that all other styles are related in some ways to Shaolin Kung Fu, thereby further confirming the value of the art they are practising.

Contrasting Shaolin and Wudang Kung Fu

Some people regard Taijiquan as a contrast to Shaolin Kung Fu: one is slow and gentle, and the other forceful and fast. But as we saw in the previous chapter, Taijiquan is derived from Shaolin, and the slow movements of Taijiquan are not an end in themselves, but are meant to develop flow of *chi* (vital energy). When Taijiquan is used for fighting, it can be very fast.

Besides Taijiquan, the other two major internal schools of Kung Fu are Bagua and Xingyi. These three schools are sometimes collectively referred to as the Wudang styles. Wudang is named after the Wudang Mountain in Hubei Province, China, where the Taoist master Zhang San Feng founded internal Kung Fu. Only Taijiquan, however, which can trace its origin back to Zhang San Feng, has any connection with Wudang Mountain; the term Wudang Kung Fu is used to cover all three internal schools mainly to contrast them with Shaolin Kung Fu.

Internal Palm of Bagua Kung Fu

The Romanized Chinese spelling 'Bagua' is pronounced and traditionally spelt as 'Pakua' in English. The founding of Bagua Kung Fu, or Baguaquan, is generally attributed to Dong Hai Chuan (1796–1880). Dong, (pronounced as 'Tung' in English), who was well-trained in Shaolin Lohan Kung Fu, reported that he was lost in a forest on the Jiu Hua Mountain, where a Taoist saint taught him a system of internal Kung Fu. Some martial arts historians suggest, although the evidence is not conclusive, that this saint could be Mi Deng Xia or Guo Ji Yuan, both of whom were classmates of the famous Wudang Taijiquan master Wang Zhong Yue. If this is true, then Bagua Kung Fu does have a historical claim to being classified as one of the Wudang arts.

The philosophy of Bagua Kung Fu is based on the Eight Trigrams of the *Yi Jing* (*I Ching*). A unique feature is that the palm is used throughout, never the fist. Hence in Chinese, Bagua Kung Fu is more popularly known as *baguazhang*, meaning 'Bagua Palm', rather than *baguaquan*, which means 'Bagua Fist'.

In Bagua Kung Fu there are eight fundamental palm techniques, corresponding to the Eight Trigrams, which multiply to give 64 techniques. The eight 'mother palms' of Bagua Kung Fu are:

- Single Changing Palm
- Double Changing Palm
- Flowing Palm

- Triple Threading Palm
- Back Palm
- Round Body Palm
- Turn Body Palm
- Return Body Palm

These terms, and those used elsewhere, may sound odd in English because they are translated literally from the Chinese; in their original form they are both meaningful and poetic.

Fig 4.1 Single Changing Palm of Bagua Kung Fu

Bagua Kung Fu is famous for its excellent footwork. Some exponents are so skilful that they can get to their opponents' backs without the latter realizing. This skill is acquired through a method called 'running round the octagonal formation of the eight trigrams', which is an essential training procedure in this style of Bagua Kung Fu.

Another typical training method of this school is *zhan zhuang*, or the art of Standing Posture, where the practitioner poses motionless in one of the eight mother palms for some time, then moves to the next step of the octagonal formation holding another pose of the mother palms. If it is practised persistently over a few years, tremendous internal force can be developed from *zhan zhuang*. It may be difficult for the uninitiated, especially those used to the hard and rough type of force training, to comprehend the profundity of this apparently simple exercise, but anyone who has had an encounter with a Bagua master can appreciate the power of his internal force.

Xingyi Kung Fu and Taoist Concepts

Xingyi (pronounced 'Hsing Yi') Kung Fu, or Xingyiquan, is reputed to have been founded by the great 12th century Song general Yue Fei, who was also a Shaolin master. Other Kung Fu historians, however, believe that although Yue Fei's military classics provided the inspiration and background material, it was the 17th century Ming Dynasty Kung Fu master, Ji Long Feng, who invented it, after witnessing an illuminating fight between a bear and an eagle.

Like Yue Fei, Ji Long Feng was an expert in the use of the spear, and he was nick-named the Super Spear. He was so skilful that he could pierce a fly resting on a paper window without damaging the paper. This is significant for Xingyi students, many of whom think that Xingyiquan is conerned only with unarmed combat.

In the past, Xingyi Kung Fu was known as Liuhequan, which means 'Kung Fu of Six Unities'. These six unities are internal force, intrinsic energy, mind, form, will-power and external strength. It was also known as Xinyiquan or shortened to Yiquan.

Xingyi means 'form' and 'mind'. The following saying reflects the meaning of Xingyiquan: 'Just internal without external cannot make good Kung Fu; just external without internal cannot make good art.' Its philosophy is based on the concept of *wu-xing*, the Five Elemental Processes – often mistranslated as the Five Elements – of metal, water, wood, fire and earth. Thus, there are five fundamental approaches which interact to create and destroy. For example, a metal approach like a chopping attack can be countered by an earth approach like a diagonal strike to the attacking arm.

The style also makes use of 12 animal forms: dragon, tiger, monkey, horse, tortoise, cockerel, hawk, swallow, snake, kite, eagle and bear. *Figure 4.2* below shows a typical Xingyi pattern.

Fig 4.2 Dragon Form of Xingyi Kung Fu

Like Bagua Kung Fu, Xingyi Kung Fu also places a great deal of emphasis on *zhan zhuang* for training internal force. Besides the motionless poses of the various animal forms, a characteristic Xingyi posture is the *sancai zhuang*, or Three Treasures Posture. If you have ever wondered why the strike of a Xingyi master can be so powerful although he may never have punched a sandbag nor lifted any weights in his training, a likely answer is that he has spent time in *zhan zhuang*.

The Philosophies of Wudang Kung Fu

It is interesting to note the philosophies behind Taijiquan and Bagua and Xingyi Kung Fu. Taiji, meaning the Grand Ultimate, is based on the principle of yin and yang, the two opposing yet complementary aspects of the reality of the whole Cosmos.

Bagua Kung Fu derives its inspiration from the *Yi Jing* (or *I-Ching*) the famous *Book of Change*, which states that the forces of yin and yang create *bagua*, the eight primordial features represented by the Eight Trigrams. Each *gua* or trigram consists of three treasures, expressed as heaven, earth and man, each represented by an unbroken yang line or a broken yin line. This classical Chinese paradigm parallels the concept in modern physics of positive and negative forces creating the proton, the electron and the neutron. The yin-yang of Taiji and the Eight Trigrams of Bagua can be combined in the symbol show in *Figure 4.3*.

The eternal interaction of the *bagua* produces 64 trigrams which symbolize the myriad features of the universe. This bagua interaction can be described by *wu-xing*, the Five Elemental Processes of metal, water, wood, fire and earth, which form the basic philosophy of Xingyi Kung Fu. The Five Elemental Processes are continuously engaged in inter-creativity and inter-destructivity as shown in *Figure 4.4*. They are governed by the forces of yin and yang, thus bringing the whole cosmic transformation into a never-ending cycle.

Fig 4.3 The combined Taiji and Bagua symbol

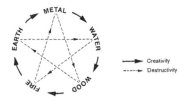

Fig 4.4 The inter-creativity and inter-destructivity of wu-xing

These philosophies of yin–yang, *bagua* and *wu-xing* are Taoist concepts. Hence, Taijiquan, Bagua Kung Fu and Xingyi Kung Fu are often considered as belonging to the Taoist school of Kung Fu, in contrast to Shaolin Kung Fu, which is Buddhist. It must be emphasized that terms like 'Buddhist' and 'Taoist' are philosophical, not religious, in meaning. Shaolin, Taijiquan, Bagua, Xingyi and all other styles of Kung Fu are non-religious: they can be practised by people of any religion without affecting their beliefs.

One should also remember that yin–yang, *bagua* and *wu-xing* represent symbolic, not absolute, concepts. Yin–yang refers to the two complementary aspects of reality, *bagua* to the eight promordial features of the universe, and *wu-xing* to the Five Elemental Processes operating the Cosmos. For example, the first *gua* or trigram is *qian*, and the second is *kun*, represented by heaven and earth respectively. *Qian* and *kun* are not actually heaven and earth, only symbolized as such. Translated into Kung Fu terms, an attack that comes from above can be regarded as a *qian* attack, whereas one that is low is a *kun* attack.

Similarly in *wu-xing*, the concept of wood creating fire suggests that a process that is characterized by growth, which is symbolized by wood, will result in activity, which is symbolized by fire. In the Kung Fu context, training that increases our force as in *zhan zhuang*, for example, will improve our attack and defence movements.

Wuzuquan or Kung Fu of Five Ancestors

As we saw in the last chapter, the classification of Kung Fu styles into external and internal is for convenience only. Wuzuquan, or Wu Chu Kung Fu, for example, is generally regarded as external, yet it has a lot of internal features. When I learned Wuzuquan from Sifu Chee Kim Thong, my most lasting memory was of my instructor constantly telling me not to use strength. How could one fight effectively, I wondered to myself, if one did not use strength? I later found that we were to use internal force.

Wuzuquan was invented by a Kung Fu genius, Bai Yi Feng, during the Yuan Dynasty (1260–1368). He invited many masters who had graduated from Shaolin Monastery back to the monastery to demonstrate their most spectacular arts. They were all specialists in their respective fields: some were experts in kicking techniques, some in agile footwork, others in internal force, and so on. Five masters, whose names have unfortunately not been recorded, were most outstanding in this display, excelling in the White Crane, Taiju, Lohan and Monkey styles and in the *chi* training of the Bodhidharma style. Bai Yi Feng combined these five styles into one, which is now known as Wuzuquan, which means 'Kung Fu of the Five Ancestors'. Later in the Ming Dynasty, Cai Yi Ming popularized this style; hence, it is sometimes known as Yi Ming Kung Fu.

Although it originated in the north, Wuzuquan became popular in southern China, especially in Fujian Province. The most important set in this style is San Zhan, meaning 'three battles', and it is used for developing internal power as much as for fighting patterns. Wuzuquan has greatly influenced Japanese karate, and San Zhan, which is known in Japanese as Sanchin, is found in many karate styles as an advanced *kata*. *Figure 4.5* shows a pattern from it.

Fig 4.5 Sinking Technique in San Zhan

Tanglangquan or Praying Mantis Kung Fu

Another popular style that is derived from Shaolin Kung Fu is Tanglangquan, or Praying Mantis Kung Fu. Wang Lang, a secular Shaolin disciple, practised Lohan Kung Fu in Shaolin Monastery during the Ming Dynasty. Partly because of his small physique, he could not beat his classmates, no matter how hard he tried.

One evening while he was resting under a tree after being beaten by his seniors in sparring, Wang Lang noticed a praying mantis fighting with a cicada. Although the praying mantis was smaller, it used its long limbs to defeat the cicada. Wang Lang was inspired. He captured a few praying mantises and studied their fighting movements, which he introduced into his Shaolin Kung Fu.

His master was amazed at his tremendous improvement, although he still could not match the best monks. With help from his master, Wang

Lang experimented with these praying mantis movements. The master suggested that he took leave from the monastery to travel the country and study other styles of martial arts. He specially advised Wang Lang to improve his footwork to refine his Praying Mantis techniques.

In his travels, Wang Lang selected the best points from 17 other Kung Fu styles to be incorporated into his Praying Mantis techniques. He found the footwork of the Monkey style the most suitable for his purpose. He called his new style Shaolin Praying Mantis Kung Fu and it is composed of the best aspects of eighteen styles:

- Taiju Long Fist
- Stretched Arm
- Bolting Method
- Short Fist
- Close Hit
- Monkey Style
- Close-Body Techniques
- Palm Strike
- Blocking Hand
- Wrestling
- Grasping
- Leaking Techniques
- Felling Techniques
- Double Kicks
- Continuous Attacks
- Straight Attacks
- Praying Mantis Techniques
- Lohan Kung Fu as Base.

He returned to Shaolin Monastery to teach Praying Mantis Kung Fu to the monks and secular disciples. It became immensely popular, and for a time it even replaced Shaolin Lohan Kung Fu as the main style in the monastery.

A Taoist master, the priest Sheng Xiao, was a regular visitor to Shaolin Monastery. One morning he was surprised to find the monks practising an odd style of Kung Fu. He was even more surprised when he could not match them with his Wudang Kung Fu.

'What's this strange Kung Fu?' he asked his friend, the Abbot of the monastery.

'It's Praying Mantis Kung Fu.'

'Praying Mantis? Aren't you ashamed that the famous monks of Shaolin are doing Praying Mantis?'

'It's an excellent art.'

'I've no doubt about that,' Sheng Xiao said. 'But what about your Shaolin Lohan Kung Fu, which has been the hallmark of Shaolin throughout the ages?'

'That's exactly my problem. I don't want to see this excellent style becoming extinct after such a short time; but I also don't want to go down in history as the Abbot who discontinued the Shaolin tradition of Lohan Kung Fu.'

Then the Shaolin Abbot and Sheng Xiao made an agreement. The

Shaolin master would teach the Taoist priest all he could about Praying Mantis Kung Fu, and Sheng Xiao promised to preserve and spread the art. So, it is an interesting feature of Praying Mantis Kung Fu that it was founded by a secular disciple, developed by Buddhist monks and popularized by a Taoist priest.

Praying Mantis Kung Fu is well known for its varied and subtle kicking techniques, an example of which is shown in *Figure 4.6*.

Fig 4.6 A Praying Mantis kick

The Spread of Southern Shaolin Kung Fu

The Qing Dynasty witnessed the growth of numerous styles from Southern Shaolin Kung Fu. In addition to the Northern Shaolin Monastery in Henan Province, another Shaolin Monastery was built in the Quanzhou district of Fujian Province during the Ming Dynasty (1368–1644). The Kung Fu taught here is referred to as Southern Shaolin Kung Fu to differentiate it from the Northern Shaolin Kung Fu of the Henan Monastery. Southern Shaolin Kung Fu is characterized by solid stances, powerful arms and elaborate hand techniques, in contrast with the elegant jumping, extensive movements and wide range of kicking attacks of the Northern Shaolin version.

The Quanzhou monastery became a centre for revolutionaries during the Qing Dynasty. According to a legend, the Qing emperor Yong Zheng himself infiltrated into the monastery as a monk to learn Shaolin Kung Fu. He later dispatched the army, aided by Tibetan lamas who were martial arts experts, to raze it. Thus, when Tibet was attacked by the Communist army and Tibetan lamas escaped to other parts of the world, some people regarded it as a karmic retribution. On the positive side, like the Shaolin masters who escaped to spread the Shaolin arts elsewhere, Tibetan lamas escaped to other parts of the world to spread Vajrayana Buddhism.

One of the Shaolin monks who escaped changed his name to Jiang Nan to avoid the pursuing army. After 50 years of wandering, with the sole aim of finding a suitable successor, he reached southern Thailand. There he met a young Kung Fu master named Yang Fa Kun who practised Fengyang Kung Fu, which is noted for the Phoenix-Eye Punch, and who earned his living as a Kung Fu display artist. The old Shaolin monk watched his display for many nights. Then one night, after the crowd had dispersed, he said to Yang Fa Kun, 'Young man, you have won a lot of applause for your display. But yours is only a display art, not real Kung Fu.'

Before Yang Fa Kun could said anything, the Venerable Jiang Nan continued, 'Don't take my word for it. The test of Kung Fu is fighting. Let's find a suitable place and have a friendly sparring match to test whether yours is a display art or real Kung Fu.'

In the subsequent sparring the Venerable Jiang Nan, who was about 80 years old, handled the 20-year-old Yang Fa Kun like a small boy. When Yang begged the monk to accept him as a student, the old Shaolin master insisted on one condition. 'Stay with me on top of a mountain and train from scratch,' he said.

About 50 years later, Yang Fa Kun taught the Shaolin arts to Ho Fatt Nam, who practised Siamese Boxing, Malay Silat and seven other styles of Kung Fu, and who earned his living as a professional Siamese Boxing fighter. Yang Fa Kun also insisted on one condition. 'You have to start from scratch,' he told Ho Fatt Nam.

I know this story intimately because Sifu Ho Fatt Nam is my master, and he generously taught me the Shaolin arts. When I begged him to accept me as a student, I already had 18 years of Kung Fu training behind me. Like his master before him, he made the one condition, 'Start from scratch'.

Major Southern Shaolin Styles

In Southern China, the five major Southern Shaolin styles were named after the families of the masters. Using these names instead of the term 'Shaolin' was one way to avoid the attention of the Qing army. These five major styles were Hongjiaquan (Hoong Family Kung Fu), Liujiaquan (Liu Family Kung Fu), Caijiaquan (Cai Family Kung Fu), Lijiaquan (Li Family Kung Fu), and Mojiaquan (Mo Family Kung Fu).

Of these five styles, Hongjiaquan is the most famous. It is often short-ened to Hongquan, which is pronounced in the same way as the Hongquan of Northern Shaolin Kung Fu described in the previous chap-ter. Hongjiaquan was named after a Shaolin master, Hong Xi Guan, and it is well known for its solid stances and powerful punches. Its form is as beautiful to watch as it is superbly effective. The teacher who first intro-duced me to Kung Fu, Sifu Lai Chin Wah, who was known in Kung Fu circles as Uncle Righteousness was a famous Hongjiaquan master.

Liujiaquan, named after Liu San Yan, is noted for its staff techniques. Caijiaquan is named after Cai Bai Da, and is famous for its kicking tech-niques. Lijiaquan is named after Li You San, and is noted for its Phoenix-Eye Punch. Mojiaquan, named after Mo Qing Jiao, is also famous for its kicks.

Some Shaolin masters specialized in particular forms which were derived from the movements and qualities of animals, such as a tiger's power and a crane's elegance. Hence, besides naming the styles after the masters, some are named after their most prominent form, such as Lung-xingquan or Dragon style Kung Fu, Heihuquan or Black Tiger Kung Fu and Paihequan or White Crane Kung Fu.

Two other popular styles of Southern Shaolin are Yongchunquan or Wing Choon Kung Fu and Cailifoquan or Choy-Li-Fatt Kung Fu.

Wing Choon Kung Fu, the style practised by the celebrated Bruce Lee, was invented by a woman, Yan Yong Chun, pronounced as Yim Wing Choon in the Cantonese dialect. It is noted for its fast movements and vicious attacks. *Figure 4.8* shows a pattern that I learned from Sifu Choe Hoong Choy.

Choy-Li-Fatt Kung Fu was invented by a patriot called Chen Heng, who combined Choy Family Kung Fu, Li Family Kung Fu and Fatt Family (or Buddha) Kung Fu into one style. It was popularized by his dis-ciple, Zhang Hung Sheng. Choy-Li-Fatt Kung Fu is remarkable for its long-reaching techniques, and its effectiveness for fighting against several attackers. *Figure 4.9* illustrates a typical Choy-Li-Fatt Kung Fu pattern.

The variety of Kung Fu styles is impressive. Each has its characteristic features and special advantages for particular needs. For example, Wing Choon Kung Fu is effective for women against brutal opponents, while Choy-Li-Fatt Kung Fu is useful for fighting one's way out of an ambush. Lohan Kung Fu takes advantage of size, whereas a large physique would be a hindrance in the Monkey style. Bagua Kung Fu uses the palm exclusive-ly, while movements of Taijiquan are performed like a poetic dance.

The styles I have described are just the major ones. There are many more, but there is not enough space to discuss them all.

Kung Fu, like any art, is a practical affair, not just a question of gathering knowledge. In other words, one becomes proficient through hard, regular practice, not by reading about it. Nevertheless, some background information is not only useful but necessary; otherwise the student may waste a lot of time groping about in the dark. The next chapter will provide you with such knowledge, so that you can derive the most benefit from your training.

Fig 4.7 A pattern from Hongjiaquan

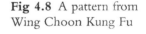

Fig 4.8 A pattern from Wing Choon Kung Fu

Fig 4.9 A pattern from Choy-Li-Fatt Kung Fu

5

DEFINING AIMS AND OBJECTIVES

Getting Better Results in a Shorter Time

❖ *With the right information, you can attain in six months what uninformed students would not attain in many years.*

The Importance of Theoretical Knowledge

While many people spend years practising Kung Fu and achieve little, some spend only a third of the time and achieve a great deal. The main reason is that while the first group learn aimlessly, usually by acquiring more and more sets without improving their force or skill, the second group know exactly what they want to get from Kung Fu and pursue their objectives accordingly. This chapter will help to place you in the élite group.

To be able to set the appropriate objectives for getting the most from your training, it is necessary to have a clear understanding of the scope and depth of Kung Fu, including its history, philosophy and various styles, as we discussed in the previous three chapters. For example, if you are unaware of the four dimensions of Kung Fu – form, force, application and philosophy – you may carry on learning sets for many years, and perhaps also teach them, but your training will be incomplete. And since form is in many ways the least important aspect of Kung Fu, you will at best achieve less than 28 per cent of what you could have done had you been more informed.

Worse still, people with this superficial knowledge may be mistaken for Kung Fu masters, especially if they are elderly, simply on the basis that they have taught the art for many years. Even if they hide nothing from their students, there is not much the students can learn apart from 'flowery fists and embroidery kicks'. Such masters may, wittingly or unwittingly, give the impression that they know much more than what they are teaching. If they are asked questions touching on the deeper aspects of Kung Fu, they would often give excuses to cover their lack of knowledge, such as that the answers are too profound or complex for the students to understand. If the students suggest sparring practice, the 'masters' may become angry and reprimand them, warning them that Kung Fu is too dangerous for them to fool around with, or that they should only practise it for their health. Students who are equally uninformed will continue learning from these teachers, and they in turn will succeed them and teach only 'flowery fists and embroidered kicks'. This is in fact what has been happening for a few generations, with the result that much of Kung Fu today has been degraded into a merely demonstrative form.

Having a theoretical understanding of Kung Fu enables you to realize that there is much more to it than merely learning form. Such an understanding will lead you, if you are still sickly, weak or nervous after some time of training, to ask why. The reasons can be traced to three factors, called the Three Requirements for Attainment, which will be explained in the next section.

Similarly, if you cannot defend yourself despite the fact that all the classics and masters have said what a marvellous martial art Kung Fu is, you have good reason to question what has gone wrong. More importantly, if you have the chance to meet great masters or read good books which expose you to the mental and spiritual aspects of great Kung Fu, you will realize that you are actually in touch with a tremendous opportunity for personal development, where effective fighting becomes comparatively petty, where health and fitness are prerequisites, and where you may expand your mind and develop your spirit until you reach the greatest achievement any person can attain, ie spiritual fulfilment.

The Three Requirements for Attainment

There are countless reasons why students fail to achieve their objectives in their Kung Fu training, but to help us understand the factors that contribute to success, great masters have from their long years of study and experience, summarized them into what are called the Three Requirements for Attainment. If you have these three requirements, you will succeed in whatever you set out to do, in Kung Fu or any other field. These three requirements are the method, the teacher and the student.

Obviously if you do not have the method you cannot even start training towards your objective. For example, you may like to acquire the art of Iron Palm, but without the method you cannot practise. If you ever acquire the Iron Palm on your own, it will be by sheer luck and will take a very long time. Morever, the result is unlikely to be as good as that developed from the proper method, and you may have harmful side-effects like deformed palms or damaged tissues. Many students try to apply their form to sparring, but without proper training methods they spar like children, even though they may have spent years learning the form and can perform sets beautifully.

There are usually different methods of achieving similar objectives. Logically, you need to seek the best available method for your abilities and needs. If you are a woman, for example, your method would probably be different from that of a man. Some martial artists proudly claim that in their art a woman can strike or block as powerfully as a strong man. She can, but she does not have to. Because of physiological, psychological and other differences (*not* inadequacies), she will take longer and need more effort to reach a high level of strength and toughness.

More important than this inefficient use of time and effort is the fact that machismo is not generally regarded as an attractive quality in a woman – and the machismo and brute force of her tough and rough mar-tial training will certainly be reflected in her daily life. It would be better for her to develop in her training those qualities at which women gener-ally excel, such as agility, fluidity and grace. Hence, she should choose a style like Shaolin Flower Fist where her natural qualities can be put to good use, rather than a style like Shaolin Lohan Kung Fu, where big mus-cles and heavy mass is an advantage.

But more important than the method is the teacher. Nowadays one can read up on many Kung Fu training methods from books, but with-out the personal instruction of a competent teacher it is difficult – though not impossible – to get good results, especially in the more advanced, inner arts. There are at least two reasons why a teacher is necessary. First the teacher can explain the finer points and overcome individual prob-lems, both of which cannot be done adequately in books. Even in a sim-ple method like the training for the Iron Palm, which basically consists of striking a sandbag with the palm, without a teacher checking on finer points like relaxing the whole arm when striking, the student may not succeed.

The second reason is, in my opinion, more important, although it is less obvious. The teacher provides the confidence students need, so that they are assured that whatever happens the teacher is around to help, sometimes even save, them. It may be difficult for people not involved in Kung Fu training to appreciate the importance of this confidence factor, but my many years of teaching both Kung Fu and Chi Kung have shown me that it is crucial. Many students, for example, have told me how easily they have achieved the desired result when they have trained with me, having already used the same method unsuccessfully for a long time. Some attributed the difference to my effective supervision, others generously said it was due to my charismatic presence. But actually it was due to the confidence I had instilled in them, so that they could totally relax and be perfectly involved in their training, without the slightest trace of doubt or worry.

For advanced arts, there is a third reason why a competent teacher is essential. Advanced skills are not taught or learned, but *transmitted* from master to student. This idea can be difficult for the uninitiated to comprehend. If you want to learn how a certain Kung Fu technique is applied in combat, for example, you can easily obtain the information from an instructor, or a book. But if you want to acquire the skill of tapping cosmic energy and channelling it to certain parts of your body, as in some advanced Shaolin Kung Fu, you have to practise the proper method together with the teacher, and at the appropriate time, when you are ready, the teacher will transmit the skill to you. Even if the instructions are written out fully and clearly, and even if you have carried them out correctly, without the master's timely initiation, it is unlikely that you will acquire the desired skill. This is one reason why in the past grateful students prostrated themselves before their teachers.

Taking time choosing a good teacher is highly recommended. Even if you have to pay a higher training fee, learning from a good teacher is always more cost- and time-effective. But what are the qualities we should look for in good teachers? Here are five guidelines.

1 They must have achieved a reasonably high standard in the art they are teaching. If they are clumsy or irritable, for instance, this indicates that they do not practise what they teach, or what they practise is not of a high standard.
2 They must be knowledgeable. If you ask how you can achieve your objectives, or any other relevant questions, they should provide satisfactory answers.
3 They should preferably be systematic and methodical, and have the means to help you accomplish your objectives. A Kung Fu expert who is haphazard and unorganized does not make a good teacher.
4 Even if they have all the other qualities, they must also be generous and willing to teach you, otherwise you must seek another teacher or try to overcome the obstacles that prevent them from teaching you.

5 The most important quality, however, the quality that distinguishes true masters, is that they teach and practise high moral values. Some people may be very competent in their art, and may even teach well, but if they swear and curse, seldom keep their word, glorify aggressive fighting or are fond of sleeping with other people's wives, it is best to steer clear of them.

The most important requirement for attainment in any art, however, is not the teacher but the student. You may have the best method and the best teacher, but if you are unwilling or not ready, you will not achieve the objectives of your training. When you have the right method and a competent teacher, what you need to do is in theory very simple: you merely have to practise regularly and persistently according to the method and teaching. But in reality, regular and persistent practice can be very difficult. Lack of practice, probably more than anything else, is the reason why many students fail in their objectives.

All the established methods of Kung Fu training have been tested over time. If an established method like Iron Shirt prescribes that you can withstand a weapon attack on your body without sustaining injury if you practise the training procedure daily for three years, it means that thousands of students in the past have tried the method and succeeded. Of course, if you practise the method daily for only three months, or only practise off and on for three years, you cannot expect to acquire the art of Iron Shirt.

It must be borne in mind that Kung Fu training is very demanding, calling for great discipline, endurance, perseverance and determination, as well as time and effort. But the result is very rewarding, and the extent of your reward depends mainly on how much purposeful practice you have put in. Aimless practice, as I said at the start of this chapter, is a waste of time. It is therefore helpful to have some idea of your aims and objectives.

Direction and Purpose

It is helpful to differentiate between aims and objectives. Aims are general in nature and long term in perspective, whereas objectives are specific and immediate. How well we have achieved our aims calls for some subjective judgement, whereas the attainment of our objectives can be determined categorically.

A major aim of Kung Fu training, for instance, is self-defence. This ability to defend ourselves is a general asset, and has long-term benefits. Generally we do not set a specific time frame for acquiring this aim; we adopt the attitude that as long as we keep on practising, we will enhance our ability to defend ourselves. We are clear that if we fail to defend ourselves effectively, it means that we failed in our aim. Sometimes we may set a time frame for our aim, but the period is usually reckoned in years rather than months. But it may not be easy for us to measure objectively how well we have achieved our aim. For example, we can say that we have achieved our aim of self-defence if we can effectively defend ourselves against street fighters; but when we are faced with a martial arts expert we may falter.

On the other hand, we may set an objective to acquire the techniques and skills to defend ourselves against kicks within six months. Hence, our objective is specific: for the time being we limit ourselves to defending ourselves against kicks, leaving defence against other types of attack to be covered by later objectives. We can go a step further and be more specific by deciding on the types of kicks we want to defend ourselves against. As we have set a time frame of six months, our objective is also immediate: we are not pursuing this objective indefinitely. We can easily decide whether we have achieved our objective within our set time. For example, after six months of practice we can ask a few classmates to kick us a number of times using the types of kicks we have defined. If we can successfully defend ourselves against all the kicks, or at least almost all of them, we can safely say we have accomplished our objective.

Although aims and objectives are closely related, an appreciation of the distinction contributes to our monitoring of our Kung Fu practice. Aims and objectives provide us with direction and purpose in our training, thus enabling us to achieve better results more quickly.

Setting Aims for Kung Fu Training

As we saw in Chapter 1, there are five major aims in practising great Kung Fu like Shaolin and Taijiquan, namely:

- self-defence
- health and fitness
- character training
- mind expansion
- spiritual development

The last two aims may not be found in most other types of Kung Fu, which are basically martial arts; Shaolin Kung Fu and Taijiquan are different because they originated not as fighting arts but as means to spiritual cultivation. They also benefit greatly from the rich and profound teachings of Buddhism and Taoism.

There are various approaches we can adopt when defining the aims of our Kung Fu training, depending on such factors as available facilities, back-up resources and our immediate needs and lifelong aspirations. We may choose only one aim and leave out the rest, consider all five but emphasize one at a time, or work towards all five simultaneously. But even if for some reason we choose only one aim, it is advisable to keep in mind all the others so that later, when the time is appropriate, we can work on them. We should regularly review our progress with reference to our set aims.

So an enthusiast who has spent a lifetime practising Kung Fu, including Taijiquan, may suddenly realize that actually it has consisted solely of 'flowery fists and embroidery kicks'. To remedy the problem, he or she may decide on self-defence as the sole aim of his or her training for the next three years, and set specific objectives to achieve that aim.

Another person, who may not be clinically sick but is nevertheless weak and languid, may choose health and fitness as the major aim of his or her training for the next two years. The objectives set for achieving this aim, as well as the methods used, will be quite different from those of the self-defence enthusiast, even though they may learn from the same teacher.

A father who is having difficulty in disciplining his boisterous son may send him to a Kung Fu master with the primary aim of giving the boy a programme of character development, with the accomplishment of other aims as a secondary consideration. A scientist or scholar may be interested in the mind expansion benefits of Kung Fu. Even if a suitable master is not immediately available, establishing this as an aim will help in the selection of a style like Shaolin Kung Fu or Taijiquan which has the potential for deeper study in the future.

The ideal martial artist with the lifelong aim of realizing his or her full potential will consider all five aims, either emphasizing one at each developmental stage, or concentrating on all of them simultaneously but gradually.

Personal Objectives

If you are lucky enough to have a good teacher, he or she will probably work out appropriate objectives with you – or *for* you often without your knowing, which in some cases may be better. When a good teacher is not available, you will have to define your own objectives to make your Kung Fu training fruitful and effective.

We may divide objectives into two categories: personal objectives and course objectives. Personal objectives are those which pertain to our personal needs, whereas course objectives are those obtained from specific courses. Ideally, your personal objectives should coincide with course objectives, ie you should be on a course that satisfies all your Kung Fu needs. But in practice you will often have to make some adjustment between your personal objectives and those of the course.

How we define our personal objectives depends on what we want to get out of our training. Understanding Kung Fu philosophy enables us to define our personal objectives wisely. One important reason why so many people get comparatively little benefit from their training, and why Kung Fu has today deteriorated into 'flowery fists and embroidery kicks' is that they are ignorant of its objectives and philosophy. If you enroll in the first Kung Fu class you come across because you are impressed with a demonstration you saw on television or because you want to get back at a neighbour who has annoyed you, you are unlikely to get the best from your training.

Personal objectives are obviously many and varied, since people's needs and aspirations, as well as their whims and fancies, are countless. The list below, which shows some wholesome personal objectives, gives an idea of the range, and may provide you with some suggestions for forming your own personal objectives.

- To find out from direct experience whether the claims made in Kung Fu classics and by Kung Fu masters are true.
- To experience, albeit in an modern context, the romance of the classical Kung Fu knights or heroes, and to be a part of a worthy tradition that is now becoming rare.
- To study a significant aspect of Eastern culture which provides a good balance to Western-style living.
- To learn an effective system for promoting health and fitness.
- To cure some illness which conventional medicine and other healing systems have not been able to remedy.

- To enjoy some form of sport or relaxation to break the dull routine of work and watching television.
- To develop Kung Fu force or skills like stamina, internal strength, fast decision-making and clarity of thought for use in daily life.
- To learn an effective means of defence against various types of attack.
- To learn additional Kung Fu techniques to enrich other forms of martial arts you already practise.
- To learn Kung Fu sets which are not only beautiful to watch but also enhance poise and movement and contribute to other arts like dancing, gymnastics and drama.
- To acquire agility and quick reflexes.
- To learn classical Kung Fu weapon sets which are exotic and not found in other martial arts.
- To find out how such tantalizing Kung Fu principles or skills as using minimum strength to overcome stronger opponents, breaking bricks without roughening the striking hand, and channelling vital energy to different parts of the body can be put into practice.
- To overcome particular emotional problems, like nervousness, indecisiveness, anxiety, depression and unreasonable fear.
- To overcome and manage stress.
- To acquire desirable emotional or mental qualities, like calmness, cheerfulness, optimism, decisiveness, clear thinking and freshness of mind.
- To acquire wholesome qualities for personal development, like humility, perseverance, determination, discipline and tolerance.
- To find out how great Kung Fu like Shaolin and Taijiquan is related to profound philosophies such as those of Buddhism and Taoism.
- To learn and practise effective techniques of meditation to expand the mind.
- To learn and practise effective methods of spiritual cultivation.

Some of the objectives mentioned above, like the first two, are fairly general, and could be classified as aims instead of as objectives. They are classified in this way for convenience, and the classification is sometimes arbitrary. I refer to them as objectives because we can put them into a time frame and measure quite decisively whether we have achieved them after training for a set period of time. For example, if after five years of Kung Fu training you find that you have become generous, righteous, courageous and helpful – the characteristics of Kung Fu knights – you can reasonably conclude you have achieved the objective of continuing the worthy tradition of those knights.

A Kung Fu knight, *xia* in Chinese, unlike his Western medieval counterpart, did not have titles conferred on him by the sovereign, nor did he necessarily kill evil dragons and save damsels from burning castles. He was a free, happy Kung Fu expert, always kind to the old and young and sometimes amorous with unattached and willing damsels. He appreciated poetry and good wine, enjoyed comfortable living whenever he could although he was often penniless because he gave away money to the poor, and was always ready to help the oppressed and suffering.

After defining a main objective, it is useful, and sometimes necessary, to draw up 'sub-objectives'. For example, if your objective is effective defence against various attacks, it is useful to define what the various attacks are, as topics for 'sub-objectives'. You may, for instance, spend three months learning to counter throws, then another three months learning how to release yourself from holds and locks.

It is necessary to set a time frame for accomplishing your objectives, and evaluate the success or otherwise of your training with direct reference to them at the end of the period. Needless to say, you must be realistic and reasonable in both your objectives and your time frames. If you can hardly perform Kung Fu form competently, for example, you cannot expect to learn enough in six months to defeat a black belt. If you are reasonable and realistic but still do not achieve your objective, you should review what had gone wrong in your training programme. This can usually be done by referring to the Three Requirements for Attainment, and asking three basic questions:

- Was my method correct?
- Was my teacher competent?
- Was I a good student?

Course Objectives

Course objectives, on the other hand, depend on the course you follow or the type of Kung Fu you practise. We may classify course objectives as elementary, intermediate and advanced. This classification, like most in Kung Fu and other disciplines, is relative and is used for the sake of easy learning. What is advanced to a student can be elementary to a master, or even to another student with a different priority and undergoing a different programme. Below are three examples taken from courses described later in the book.

Course: Shaolin Five Animals
Level: Elementary (for students)
Time: Six months of daily practice

OBJECTIVES:
1 to become familiar with some of the basic patterns and fundamental movements of Shaolin Kung Fu
2 to be introduced to sequences of patterns performed continuously, with reference to breath control and related application
3 to perform a Kung Fu set with accuracy of form, force and speed
4 to lay the foundation for applying the patterns in the set, individually or in sequence, for combat
5 to lay the foundation for studying Kung Fu principles and other theoretical information related to the patterns and set

Course: Combat Application of Shaolin Five Animals
Level: Intermediate (for students)
Time: One year of daily practice

OBJECTIVES:
1 to learn and practise the combat application of the individual patterns of the Shaolin Five Animals set
2 to learn some useful variations from the application
3 to apply relevant patterns as specific techniques against particular combat situations
4 to acquire the foundation for progressing from specific techniques to combat sequences
5 to learn and practise combat skills like spacing, timing, balance and fluidity of movement
6 to lay the foundation for studying relevant Kung Fu principles and other theoretical information related to combat application

Course: Abdominal Breathing
Level: Advanced (for students)
Time: One year of daily practice

OBJECTIVES:
1 to be introduced to Shaolin Chi Kung
2 to learn and practise a fundamental Chi Kung breathing technique
3 to develop a field of energy at the abdomen
4 to apply this collected vital energy to Kung Fu as well as to daily life
5 to apply the breath control technique as a means of deep meditation

The advantage of practising Kung Fu with an awareness of course objectives over random practice is obvious. Yet most people, mainly because of lack of theoretical information, practise arduously without knowing clearly why they do so, or what benefits they expect. They practise a set, usually because it is the one that their instructor teaches, without knowing why the patterns are chosen to form the set, or why they are linked in that particular way. As a result, despite their devotion to Kung Fu and their practice of the set for many years, their attainment, both in terms of skill and knowledge, is not much higher than that of their first year.

With the right information, you can attain in six months what uninformed students would not attain in many years. If you are successful in accomplishing the course objectives of the set mentioned above, for example, you will understand the significance of the patterns in the set, the specific techniques and combat sequences, and the relevant Kung Fu principles. You will also be able to regulate your breathing and perform the set accurately with some force and reasonable speed.

With the philosophical preparation provided so far we are now ready to proceed to practical work.

6

THE FOUNDATION OF SHAOLIN KUNG FU

Hand Forms, Stances and Basic Patterns

❖ *Today when you learn a Shaolin Kung Fu set, which incorporates numerous patterns with different hand forms and stances, you inherit the crystallization of hundreds of years of Kung Fu development.*

Inheritance from Past Masters

Through the centuries Kung Fu masters have discovered that certain methods of attack or defence had certain advantages in particular combat situations. For example, they found that by punching out from waist level they could execute more power than from shoulder level. By maintaining good balance they could execute kicks more accurately and forcefully than if they were unbalanced. By moving their hands in a circular way, they could minimize their opponent's force when blocking punching attacks. By shifting their body backward in a particular stance, they could avoid the opponent's kicks without having to move their legs back. These movements, which gave them technical advantages in combat, were stylized into what are now called Kung Fu patterns.

The earliest Kung Fu patterns were discovered through long years of trial and error. Later, when the early masters had accumulated enough patterns of many different kinds to formulate principles and theories, study and experimentation played a more important role in the invention of more patterns. For example, through trial and error they discovered that, in addition to a straight punch from the waist, they could also strike an opponent using their swinging arms, or with an elbow. They also discovered that striking an opponent with a swinging arm was desirable only if their arms were strong and the opponent was relatively far away. If their arms were not sufficiently strong, or if the opponent was very close, an elbow strike would be more effective. In this way they gradually developed a body of principles and theories for combat, and when these were established, they could invent more patterns and formulate more principles, not necessarily from actual fighting but from study and speculation, and from experimentation with their students.

The early masters also learned some invaluable lessons by observing the behaviour and movements of animals and birds. Do not underrate these creatures: except in brain power, we humans are actually far behind animals and birds in many aspects of bodily functions, sensual perception and instinct for survival. The power of a tiger, the endurance of an ox and the sharpness of an eagle are proverbial. Even small creatures surpass humans in many qualities essential to martial artists. A rabbit or a squirrel, for instance, can sense approaching danger accurately and move away with great dexterity and agility. Hence, early masters not only invented Kung Fu patterns based on the swift and effective movements of the animals and birds, but also drew inspiration from their characteristics to devise training methods to develop abilities like a tiger's power and a rabbit's dexterity.

These patterns and skills have been accumulated and improved upon throughout the ages, and passed on from generation to generation. Shaolin Monastery was the first known institution to study and promote this accumulation of forms, skills and information in a systematic, professional way, and has remained the leading authority in this field ever since. Thus, Kung Fu reached a very fine level. For example, while many martial arts mainly employ the clenched fist, there are about 20 forms for attacking with the hand in Shaolin Kung Fu. While some martial arts pay little attention to the way their practitioners stand, Shaolin Kung Fu places a lot of emphasis on stances, of which there are more than a dozen types. The reason for such detail is that, depending on the combat situation in question, a particular way of holding the hand in a particular stance in both attack and defence gives the exponent certain technical advantages. Thus, today when you learn a Shaolin Kung Fu set, which incorporates numerous patterns with different hand forms and stances, you inherit the crystallization of hundreds of years of Kung Fu development.

The Significance of Form and Formlessness

For a beginner, Shaolin Kung Fu patterns, with their various hand forms and stances are 'unnatural'. In a combat situation, for example, it is unnatural for a person unfamiliar with Shaolin Kung Fu to stand in a

Bow-Arrow Stance and thrust out a straight punch in a pattern known as Black Tiger Steals Heart, a very common Shaolin pattern. It would be more 'natural' to stand as in judo, or to punch as in Western boxing. But this 'unnatural' pattern has many technical advantages over an ordinary punch. For instance, using the Black Tiger Steals Heart pattern generates more power in the punch and greater balance in the stance. So, in order to benefit from these advantages, the practitioner has to learn the pattern which is initially unnatural, and practise it so well that it eventually becomes natural to him.

In the early stages the student must learn and practise Kung Fu patterns exactly, paying careful attention to correctness of form. This is the stage of 'from formlessness to form', meaning that initially the student has no Kung Fu form, but with persistent practice it becomes second nature.

At a later stage when one is competent in the form, one may if necessary modify it to suit the demands of a particular combat situation. For example, instead of keeping the body upright in the Bow-Arrow Stance when executing the Black Tiger punch – a form one must follow strictly when first learning and practising it – one may later, if the situation warrants it, slant the body slightly forward to achieve a longer reach with the punch. This approaches the stage of 'from form to formlessness', meaning that after having mastered the standard form, one is now not bound by its details; within the general mode of the form, one can move the hands, legs or any parts of the body in any way appropriate to the situation. At an advanced stage, one may even do away with form, because one's strike is so fast and powerful that however one moves, one defeats one's opponent. It is similar to an adult fighting with a three-year-old child: the adult need not bother with any Kung Fu form; he or she is so comparatively powerful that the child simply has no chance.

A student, however, needs to know Kung Fu form, which is acquired through the practice of patterns and sets. But before you can perform Shaolin Kung Fu patterns and sets well, you must know how to hold your hands correctly in the basic Shaolin hand forms, and stand firmly in good balance in the basic Shaolin stances.

Various Shaolin Hand Forms

'A picture is worth a thousand words', *Figures 6.1* and *6.2* show a variety of Shaolin hand forms:

1 Level Fist
2 Sun-Character Fist, or Vertical Fist
3 Leopard Punch
4 Phoenix-Eye Fist
5 Elephant Fist
6 Willow–Leaf Palm
7 Dragon Palm
8 Dragon Hand Form
9 Tiger Claw
10 Eagle Claw
11 Snake Hand
12 One-Finger Zen
13 Sword Finger
14 Crab Pincers
15 Crane Beak
16 Monkey Paw
17 Praying Mantis Hand
18 Hook Hand

| Level fist | Sun-character fist | Leopard punch | Phoenix-eye punch |

| Willow-leaf palm | Dragon palm | Dragon hand-form | Tiger claw | Eagle claw |

Fig 6.1 Shaolin hand forms 1–9

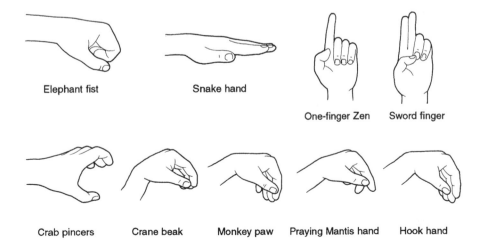

| Elephant fist | Snake hand | One-finger Zen | Sword finger |

| Crab pincers | Crane beak | Monkey paw | Praying Mantis hand | Hook hand |

Fig 6.2 Shaolin hand forms 10–18

Some of these hand forms are the primary way of holding the hands in their respective Kung Fu styles. For example, in the Monkey style and Praying Mantis Kung Fu respectively, the Monkey Paw and the Praying Mantis Hand are extensively used. The Crane Beak and the Hook Hand appear similar, but they are actually different in function. As their names imply, the Crane Beak, mainly found in Souther Shaolin Kung Fu, is used for 'beaking', for example on the opponent's vital points, whereas the Hook Hand, mainly found in Northern Shaolin Kung Fu, is for 'hooking', for example on the opponent's leg.

The richness of Shaolin Kung Fu is reflected in the fact that a dozen striking techniques can be executed with the Level Fist. *Figures 6.3–6.5* show these techniques.

1 Straight Punch	5 Sweeping Punch	9 Hanging Punch
2 Cannon Punch	6 Whip Punch	10 Sinking Punch
3 Horn Punch	7 Wave Punch	11 Armpit Punch
4 Diagonal Punch	8 Chopping Punch	12 Throwing Punch

Straight punch

Canon punch

Horn punch

Swinging punch

Fig 6.3 Techniques of the Level Fist (1–4)

Fig 6.4 Techniques of the Level Fist (5–8)

Fig 6.5 Techniques of the Level Fist (9–12)

The other hand forms are not so extensive in their striking techniques.

Horseriding and Other Stances

Figures 6.6–6.9 show the many stances in Shaolin Kung Fu.

1 Horseriding Stance
2 Bow-Arrow Stance
3 False-Leg Stance
4 Unicorn Step Stance
5 Ring Step
6 Single-Leg Stance
7 Side-Body Stance
8 Slanting-Body Stance
9 J-Character Stance

10 Stream-Character or Four-Six Stance
11 Triangle Stance
12 Two-Character Stance
13 Goat Stance
14 Seven-Star Step
15 Front-Arrow Stance
16 Half-Kneel Step
17 Single-Shield Step
18 Cat Step

Horse riding

Bow – arrow

False leg

Fig 6.6 Shaolin stances (1–3)

It is sufficient at this stage to know how to perform the hand forms and stances correctly. Apart from the Horseriding Stance which is explained below, their actual practice can commence when they appear in Kung Fu patterns. (Some of these hand forms and stances, like the Praying Mantis Hand and Stream-Character Stance, are not shown in patterns in this book, although they are popular in some special styles of Kung Fu.)

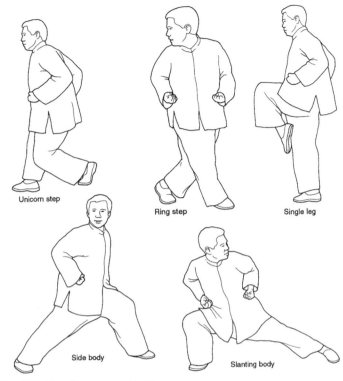

Unicorn step

Ring step

Single leg

Side body

Slanting body

Fig 6.7 Shaolin stances (4–8)

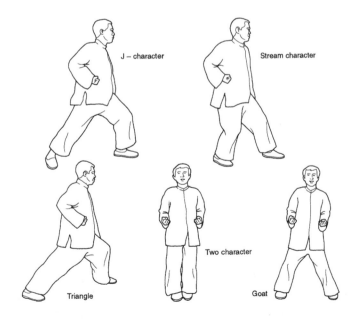

J – character

Stream character

Triangle

Two character

Goat

Fig 6.8 Shaolin stances (9–13)

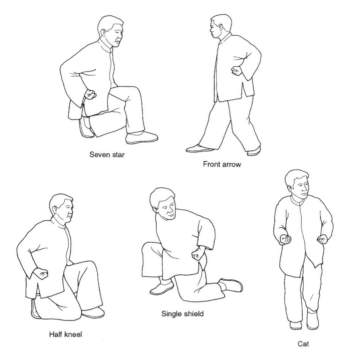

Seven star

Front arrow

Half kneel

Single shield

Cat

Fig 6.9 Shaolin stances (14–18)

The Horseriding Stance is the most important in Shaolin Kung Fu, especially Southern Shaolin. If you are serious in learning good Shaolin Kung Fu, it is strongly recommended that you practise this stance for at least a few months before beginning Kung Fu proper, as students did in the past. Alternatively you should practise this stance for at least two weeks, then continue to practise it for a few months while you also learn other Kung Fu forms.

There are good reasons why it is so important. The stances constitute the foundation upon which Kung Fu patterns are built, and the Horseriding Stance is the 'mother' stance; the force and skill derived from it enable you to perform the other stances well. It builds strength in your legs; it replaces your 'old' strength with a new strength with which you can, besides other benefits, break bricks with kicks and walk for miles without feeling tired. At certain times, when your old strength has been drained but the new strength has not been built up, your legs may be very weak and you may have difficulty even going up the stairs. Do not worry; this is a normal development and your legs will be strong after a few days.

The Horseriding Stance training also lowers your centre of gravity from somewhere at your chest to the level of your abdomen, making you 'fresh on top, and stable below', meaning you are alert and well balanced, both physically and mentally. These two qualities, more than the techniques you will learn later, are the marks of a Kung Fu master. And finally, the training builds a ball of vital energy in your abdominal *dan tian*, or energy field. Only when you have sufficient vital energy in your *dan tian* can you effectively train for internal force, because it is the source from which internal force flows.

The Horseriding Stance is a very demanding form of *zhan zhuang* (standing posture) Chi Kung, but it is worth all the time and effort practising it. One reason why many students do not become masters even after they have trained for a long time is that they lack this source of vital energy in their *dan tian*, and this lack can be traced to insufficient training in whatever forms of *zhan zhuang* their styles of Kung Fu prescribe.

Here are a few helpful points for your Horseriding Stance training. Your body should be upright, and your thighs almost parallel to the ground. You must take care not to raise your body when you are tired – something most beginners inevitably do without realizing it. Although there may be some tension resulting from your posture, relax your mind and body. Focus your mind on your abdomen. Your eyes may be open or closed, but you must not think of anything. Most people cannot hold this stance for a minute, but you must persevere until you can hold it correctly for at least five minutes if you want to benefit from it. You probably need about three months of daily practice to achieve this minimum requirement.

You can if you wish change to other stances, like the Bow-Arrow Stance (where the body weight is distributed equally between two legs) and the False-Leg Stance (where the back leg supports more than 95 per cent of the body weight), when you become tired from sitting in the Horseriding Stance. Simply turn your body and change your foot position without coming out of your stance. Change back to the Horseriding Stance when you are ready for another round of endurance. Spend some time too on the Single-Leg Stance and the Unicorn Step (where the distribution of weight is about 60 per cent in front and 40 per cent at the back). These five stances are frequently used in Shaolin Kung Fu, and are therefore called the basic stances.

After stance training, you must practise leg-stretching exercises so that your legs will be not only strong and solid but also agile and supple. *Figures 6.10* and *6.11* show six such exercises, which are collectively known in our Kung Fu school, Shaolin Wahnam Kung Fu, as the Art of Flexible Legs. (This is a general name; other schools may use different sets of exercises to stretch their legs.) Perform each exercise about 10–20 times.

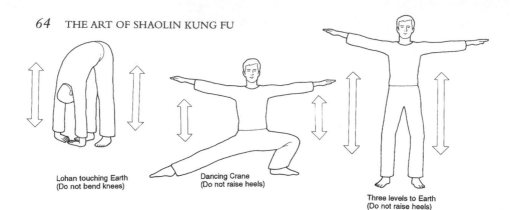

Lohan touching Earth
(Do not bend knees)

Dancing Crane
(Do not raise heels)

Three levels to Earth
(Do not raise heels)

Fig 6.10 Leg-stretching exercises (1–3)

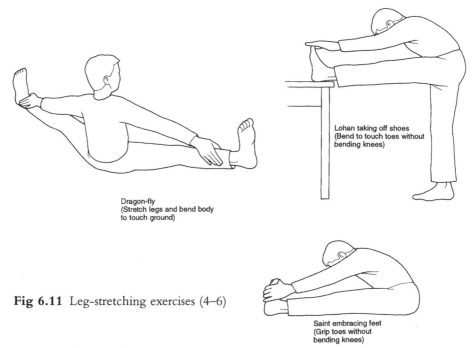

Lohan taking off shoes
(Bend to touch toes without
bending knees)

Dragon-fly
(Stretch legs and bend body
to touch ground)

Fig 6.11 Leg-stretching exercises (4–6)

Saint embracing feet
(Grip toes without
bending knees)

Basic Shaolin Patterns

When you are familiar with the Shaolin hand forms and stances, you can proceed to learn the following eight simple patterns. In Shaolin Kung Fu every pattern has a meaningful, poetic name, usually in four characters. The names of the eight patterns are as follows, although the poetry is often lost in the translation. You can practise their form by referring to *Figures 6.12–6.15.*

1 Black Tiger Steals Heart
2 Single Tiger Emerges from Cave
3 Poisonous Snake Shoots Venom

4 Beauty Looks at Mirror
5 Precious Duck Swims Through Lotus
6 False-Leg Hand Sweep
7 Golden Star at Corner
8 Immortal Emerges from Cave

Fig 6.12 Shaolin Kung Fu patterns 1 and 2

Black Tiger steals heart

Single Tiger emerges from cave

Fig 6.13 Shaolin Kung Fu patterns 3 and 4

Poisonous Snake shoots venom

Beauty looks at mirror

Fig 6.14 Shaolin Kung Fu patterns 5 and 6

Precious Duck swims through Lotus

False leg hand sweep

Fig 6.15 Shaolin Kung Fu patterns 7 and 8

Golden Star at corner

Immortal emerges from cave

Learn only one pattern at a time, and practise it many times until you are quite familiar with its form before proceeding to the next pattern. Remember that the essence of Kung Fu training is developing force and skill, which in this case is an ability to perform the patterns correctly and dextrously, and not acquiring more and more forms.

The figures show only either the left-hand or the right-hand form of each pattern, but you should practise both forms many times. Initially, you should start from the Ready Position, which is just standing upright and relaxed, with both fists at the waist. Perform the pattern, then return to the Ready Position. Later you may start and end in any position.

Initially you should practise the patterns in the sequence shown, but later you can practise them in any order. It usually takes a beginner about three months of daily practice to be able to perform the patterns well, with each practice session lasting about half an hour.

As I said in the last chapter, it is important to define the aims and objectives of your Kung Fu training if you want to get the best results in the shortest time. It would be a good idea to spend three months of daily practice on stances and patterns, and call the course 'The Foundations of Shaolin Kung Fu'. The term 'foundations' indicates that your future success depends very much on how well you perform these basic stances and patterns. So even if you are experienced in other martial arts but new to Shaolin Kung Fu, it is advisable to spend three months on them.

The main aim of this course, naturally, is to provide a sound foundation for your later development in Shaolin Kung Fu, and this includes the information on why training in the Horseriding Stance is important, why different hand forms and stances are employed, and why you should spend time in solo pattern practice. (If you are still unsure of the answers, you would do well to read this chapter again.)

The course objectives are to be aware of the variety of hand forms and stances in Shaolin Kung Fu, to be able to perform the basic stances and patterns properly, to lower the body's centre of gravity for better balance, and to accumulate vital energy in the abdominal *dan tian* to prepare for future internal force training.

You should define your own personal objectives according to your own abilities, needs, aspirations and other relevant factors. The following are just some suggestions:

- to sit in the Horseriding Stance for at least five minutes
- to walk 10 miles without feeling tired
- to execute all of the basic patterns flawlessly
- to complete three rounds of all the basic patterns continuously without feeling tired

At the end of your course, you should evaluate the success or otherwise of your training with direct reference to your course and personal objectives.

7

FROM FORM TO COMBAT APPLICATION

Developing Specific Techniques and Combat Skills

❖ *These specific techniques are an effective means of preparing for sparring.*

The Four Directions of Attack

When you can perform the eight basic Shaolin patterns described in the previous chapter proficiently, the next step is to learn and practise their combat application. If you examine the eight patterns, you may notice three significant points. For those with some experience in martial arts, it is not difficult to see the first two: all the eight patterns involve hand techniques, and they are arranged in attack–defence combinations. This may also give you a clue to the third point: why those four pairs of attack–defence patterns were chosen.

The four pairs represent four directions of attack and their defence. Of course, attacks can come from any direction, but they may be generalized into four main positions: top, middle, bottom and sideways. If you can defend yourself efficiently against the four basic hand attacks from these four directions, you can defend yourself from any other hand attacks of similar kinds from any direction.

Let us take the first pair of attack–defence patterns as an illustration. The Black Tiger Punch is an attack to the middle using a Level Fist; its defence is a leaning block using a Tiger Claw. If you can effectively defend yourself against this attack, you can defend yourself against any similar attacks, irrespective of whether the attacker uses a Level Fist, or another hand form like a Phoenix-Eye Fist, a Willow-Leaf Palm or a Leopard Punch. Similarly, if you can effectively defend yourself against the top attack, the bottom attack, and the side attack – represented in the basic attack patterns as a Snake Hand to the throat, a low-level punch to the abdomen and a Horn Punch to the temple – you can also defend yourself from all other similar attacks to your top, bottom and sides, even if the opponent changes his stance and hand form.

Conversely, if you are proficient in the four basic hand attacks, you can increase your modes of attack by varying your hand forms and stances. Thus, by learning and practising these eight basic patterns, you will be able to defend yourself against many types of hand attacks from any direction.

The four basic defence patterns also illustrate an important Kung Fu principle: to use different modes of defence according to the modes of attack, so that you can get the best advantage from the situation. You should not use the same method of blocking, for example, irrespective of how your attacker strikes you. Another Kung Fu principle advises: if the strike aims at your top, float it; if it aims at your middle, lean against it; if it aims at your bottom, sweep it; and if it comes from the sides, intercept it. These four defence techniques – floating, leaning, sweeping and intercepting – are represented in the four basic defence patterns you have learned, and will be further explained in their respective patterns latter.

An Imaginary Opponent in Skill Training

In Kung Fu, knowing how to attack and defend is not enough; you have to practise and practise until your attack and defence become second nature to you. Remember that the aim of Kung Fu is not just gathering knowledge (although knowledge is important), but developing force and skill.

Initially, however, you need not – indeed *should* not – practise the attack-defence patterns with a partner; you should practise on your own, visualizing an imaginary opponent. There is a lot of difference between solo practising of the attack-defence patterns as you did in the previous chapter, and using the same patterns in combat applications, even with training partners. If you find this hard to believe, try it out yourself by asking someone to attack you using some *pre-determined* patterns. Even when you know what types of attack are coming, and how you should defend against them, you will be hesitant in your movements, mistaken in your judgement, staccato in your reaction or clumsy in your balance. And you will have a better idea why many Kung Fu students who have learned Kung Fu form for a long time but have never practised sparring methodically fight like children, even in a competition ring.

What many people are unaware of is that fighting involves not only techniques, but more significantly skills like anticipation, timing, spacing and fluidity of movement, which have to be developed methodically. What you have done in the course on the Foundation of Shaolin Kung Fu (see Chapter 6) is to learn the techniques of basic attack and defence (with some skill to perform them well), but not yet the skills for simulated or actual combat. So you should go over these attack–defence patterns again, but this time with an imaginary opponent in mind.

'But why can't I have a training partner to act as my opponent?' you may ask. 'Isn't a training partner more realistic than an imaginary opponent?' The reason is that your immediate task is not realistic sparring, but developing combative skills. It is much easier and more convenient to train on your own with an imaginary opponent, because in this way you can control and regulate such crucial factors as the attacking pattern the 'opponent' uses, the spacing between you, and how fast the attack is. It is the repeated practice in responding to these factors, which you can better manipulate with an imaginary opponent, that develops in you skills like anticipation, spacing and timing. At the appropriate time in your progress, you can visualize your imaginary opponent changing pace, position or attack–defence patterns, thus enabling you to develop skills like making split-second decisions, appropriate responses and fluidity of movement as you adjust to the changes. In this way you will develop an invaluable skill: you will train your body to respond instantaneously to your thoughts. A training partner cannot supply this kind of training; even if someone is willing to carry out all your requests, it is too cumbersome and impracticable to keep telling him or her what to do.

When you have acquired the combat skills, *then* you should get a partner to train with you. You will find that if you have prepared yourself well with an imaginary opponent, it is easy to handle training partners or real opponents (unless they are far above your level), because they are usually less adroit than your imaginary opponent. Even if you do not have a partner to practise with, your training with your imaginary opponent can develop you to a fairly high level so that when you meet a real opponent who attacks you in the way you have trained yourself, you will have an efficient defence.

Defence patterns which have been devised to overcome specific combat situations – in this case hand attacks to the top, middle, bottom and sides – are called specific techniques. So, you have now learned four specific techniques for four specific combat situations. The next section will help you in your practice.

The Principles of Effective Combat

Start and end each attack and defence pattern with a poise pattern, such as Lohan Asks the Way or Single Tiger Emerges from Cave, which can also be used for attack or defence. In the poise pattern, the exponent places one hand in front as a guard. The attacker must push the defender's guarding hand away or down as he or she attacks, known respectively as 'opening the way' and 'taming the hand'. Opening the way is to open the opponent's defence; taming the hand is to press one hand over the opponent's hand to minimize the opportunity for counter-attack.

Figure 7.1 shows the poise patterns and the various attack-defence combinations. It is, of course, not easy to learn these movements from a book; beginners are strongly recommended to learn from Kung Fu instructors. Even if you learn a Kung Fu style different from the one taught here, having some practical experience will enable you to follow these movements better. The diagrams show only the left or the right mode of attack and defence; you should practise both.

Top attack

Middle attack

Low attack

Side attack

Fig 7.1 Specific techniques for hand attacks

In your practice with a training partner, pay attention to getting the form, balance and fluidity of movement right, rather than trying to defeat the other. If one is slow or hesitant, the other should slow down to adjust to

his or her partner's speed or skill; the objective is to co-operate for your
mutual benefit, not to outdo each other. Reverse roles as attacker and
defender so that you can both appreciate how an opponent would feel
and act. Make sure that even if the defender fails to respond correctly, the
attacker does not hit him or her; the strike should stop a few inches from
target.

In the Poisonous Snake attack, the attacker aims at the defender's
throat. Remember to open the way or tame the defender's hand before
moving in to attack. Make sure that the spacing is correct; if the strike is
successful it will connect, but in practice it should stop a few inches from
the target. The defender moves one leg backwards and blocks the attack
with Beauty Looks at Mirror, which is frequently called a Mirror Hand.
Pay attention to your timing; do not move prematurely, as many novices
do, irrespective of how long they may been have learning Kung Fu.
Notice that the Mirror Hand floats the attacking arm, following the
attacking momentum, enabling you to use less force to block a powerful
attack. You may, if the situation is favourable, counter-strike your opponent after the block, but you must also be prepared for the fact that he or
she may follow with a second attack. But in this practice, you need not
worry about the follow up action yet; the main purpose here is to develop combat skills like timing, spacing, balance and fluidity of movement.

In the Black Tiger attack, the attacker aims at the defender's heart. But
you must stop a few inches away from the target if your partner fails to
respond correctly. The defender moves a small step backward to stand at
the False-Leg Stance and responds with Single Tiger Emerges from Cave.
(This defence pattern is the same Single Tiger pattern but using a different hand if the defender also uses Single Tiger Emerges from Cave as a
poise pattern.) This kind of blocking technique is known as leaning; the
defender gracefully 'leans' his or her arm on the attacker's arm, and does
not brutally ward it off. You do not have to use much strength in your
blocking, because as you have moved away from the attack by stepping
slightly backwards, it could not reach you even if you do not block.
Immediately after leaning, lower your Tiger Claw to grip the attacker's
elbow or wrist. At this instant the defender becomes the attacker, and vice
versa. A master who specializes in the art of Tiger Claw can immobilize
an aggressor by one grip on vital points of the arm. If you are a student,
concentrate on the leaning and leave the complexity of the Tiger Claw
grip for later development.

In the third combination the attacker, after having opened or tamed
the defender's guarding hand, moves in with a low Precious Duck punch.

The defender steps back and counters with False-Leg Hand Sweep. Notice that this is not meant to ward off the attack; as he has moved away from the attack it would not reach him even if he did not sweep down his hand. The Hand Sweep is meant to strike the attacker's arm, preferably at his wrist or elbow, at the time when the attacking arm is fully spent. It is amazing how effectively such an apparently simple pattern can implement an advanced and fairly difficult principle, namely that 'the golden time to strike is when the opponent's old strength is spent, and before any new strength is generated'. In one simple stroke, a master can break or dislocate an attacker's arm before the latter realizes what has happened.

These three Defence patterns illustrate three levels of defence technique:

1 Defence followed by counter
2 Defence and counter combined
3 No defence, direct counter

At the elementary level, the exponent first defends against the attacking move, then follows up with a counter-attack. This is a safe technique, with the avoidance of injury as the top priority. At the intermediate level, the exponent executes the defence and counter-attack patterns as if they were one continuous pattern. This is also a safe technique because it ensures that the attack is under control, even if only momentarily, before counter-attacking – although the counter-attack is so fast and follows the defence so naturally that the opponent finds no break in between.

At the advanced level, it appears as though the exponent does not bother to defend against the attack and counter attacks directly, although the defence actually takes the form of a body movement or other method. It is also a safe technique, but it demands a lot of skill and knowledge, and is therefore generally not advisable for beginners. However, even though it incorporates an advanced technique, this Hand Sweep pattern is simple enough for even beginners to execute.

All defence techniques in Shaolin Kung Fu must be safe; it is a basic principle that an exponent must first be sure of his or her own safety before considering any counter-attack. Exchanging blows generously, which is not uncommon in some other martial arts, is unthinkable in Shaolin philosophy, because a Shaolin disciple always assumes that an opponent is competent and able to inflict damage with just one blow.

In the fourth combination, the attacker moves in to strike the defender's head with a Horn Punch. It is normally not a good attacking move, because the range is short (thus the attacker has to be close to the defender), and the attacker's body is exposed. But a competent exponent may use it as a bait, especially if one deliberately leaves one's body unguarded by the other hand, to tempt the opponent to counter-attack so that one can follow up the counter-attack. *Figure 7.2* shows two such surprise follow-ups, one using defence and counter together and the other no defence, but a direct counter.

So, to be safe, the defender blocks the attack with the Immortal pattern. The blocking action is an upward movement to float the attack, rather than a direct clash with the oncoming arm. You will have a better idea of this if you imagine yourself to be a giant leaving a small cave; you push your hand towards the cave roof to prevent your head knocking on it. In this pattern, you must also be careful of the attacker's other hand.

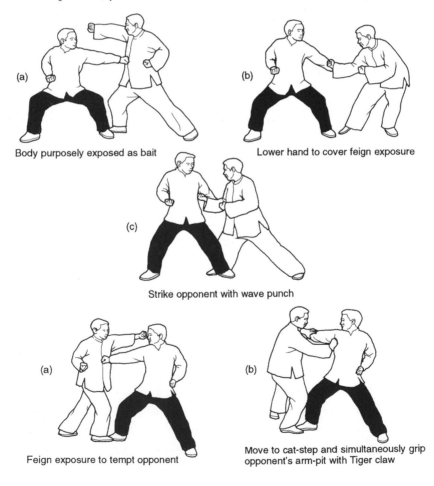

(a) Body purposely exposed as bait

(b) Lower hand to cover feign exposure

(c) Strike opponent with wave punch

(a) Feign exposure to tempt opponent

(b) Move to cat-step and simultaneously grip opponent's arm-pit with Tiger claw

Fig 7.2 Surprise counters following a bait

In your specific technique training, you need not worry about the advanced follow-up patterns; just focus on the simple patterns to develop combat skills. You should spend at least three months of daily practice on this course, which we will call 'Specific Techniques for Hand Attacks', including at least a month (preferably more) with your imaginary opponent. The course objectives include learning and practising specific techniques for countering four basic hand attacks, acquiring the combat skills of anticipation, timing, spacing, balance and fluid movement, and understanding important principles of combat like safety first, the four directions and the three levels of defence. You should devise your own personal objectives.

Specific Techniques Against Kicks

When you are quite competent in your defence against the four basic hand strikes, you should proceed to defence against other categories of attack, of which there are four:

- strikes, especially with the hands but also include striking with the head, shoulders, elbows, thighs and back, and 'dotting' with the fingers
- kicks, especially with the feet, but also with the knees and shins
- Falls, ie various ways of felling opponents, including doing so without using the hands
- Holds and grips, especially gripping vital points, but also including gripping muscles and tendons, and immobilizing joints

The variety of Shaolin Kung Fu patterns for attack and defence is bewildering. Although many people may not be aware of it, there are actually more kicks, felling techniques and holds and grips in Shaolin Kung Fu than in all the other world famous martial arts put together! All the kicks found in Taekwondo and Siamese Boxing, all the throws found in judo, and all the holds found in Aikido are also found in Shaolin Kung Fu, but there are kicks, felling techniques and holds not found in them, well known though they are for their different kinds of attack. As far as I know, the Horse's Back Kick and Dragonfly Kick, for example, are not found in any other martial arts; throws are only one of the 18 major techniques for felling opponents in Shaolin Kung Fu, whereas the others, such as Leg Sweep and Shoulder Push, are not found in judo. *Figure 7.3* shows some unique Shaolin Kung Fu techniques.

Fairy looking at shadow

Reverse kicking of purple bell

Lie in sea looking at the sky

Two dragons playing with pearl

Fig 7.3 Some unique techniques of Shaolin Kung Fu

There is not enough space to give a detailed description of all these techniques here, but I have choosen four basic kicks and their counters to explain in one set, and two felling techniques and two holds and their counters in another.

As in the set of specific techniques explained earlier, you should first practise the attack and defence patterns individually. You should have kicked a total of at least 1,000 times for each kicking pattern before attempting its combat application. Then practise with your imaginary opponent and finally with a training partner. When training with a partner, take great care not to hurt each other accidentally. Focus on developing skills, not just on learning the form.

Figure 7.4 shows the kicking attacks and their defence, and *Figure 7.5* their application. The names of the attack and defence patterns are as follows.

1 Kicking the Sky
2 Tame Tiger with Beads
3 Happy Bird Hops up Branch
4 Lohan Strikes Drum
5 Yellow Oriole Drinks Water
6 Cut Bamboo with Branches
7 Naughty Monkey Kicks Tree
8 Swimming Dragon Plays with Water

Kicking the sky

Tame Tiger with beads

Happy bird hops up branch

Lohan strikes drum

Yellow Oriole drinks water

Cut bamboo
with branch

Naughty Monkey kicks tree

Swimming Dragon plays with water

Fig 7.4 Kicking attacks and their defence

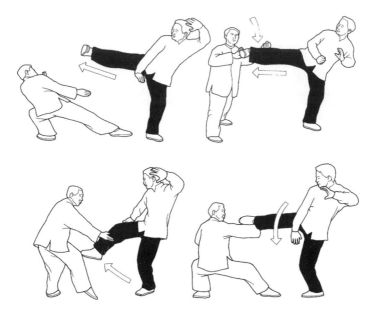

Fig 7.5 Application of kicking techniques

High kicks like Kicking the Sky are discouraged in Shaolin Kung Fu because they expose the vulnerable sex organ to risky counter attacks. It is shown here for practice only, and you are strongly advised not to use such high kicks in combat unless you have a good reason to do, such as when an opponent holding a dagger jumps up high in the air to attack you. If a Shaolin master wants to kick your head, he usually does so while he is in the air, with his other leg covering his organ, and not while he is on the ground. One easy way to avoid a high kick executed from the ground is to lower and slant your body backward without having to move your legs, as in the pattern Tame Tiger with Beads.

Middle side kicks like Happy Bird Hops up Branch are frequently used in Shaolin Kung Fu. One hand must cover the sex organ when executing the kick, and the leg must be withdrawn immediately after kicking, or else it might be hit by the defender using the counter Lohan Strikes a Drum as in this attack-defence combination. Notice that the defender has moved his body backwards to the sideways Bow-Arrow Stance so that he will not be hit even if the attacker continues a few more fast kicks from his position, unless he has dropped his kicking leg and moved close to the defender.

Yellow Oriole Drinks Water, in the third attack-defence combination, represents one of the patterns in the famous Shaolin kicking technique called No-Shadow Kicks. The striking point of the kick is the instep, and the kick aims at the sex organ. It is, therefore, also called Organ-Seeking Kick. Out of consideration Shaolin disciples usually kick higher at the opponent's abdomen, so as not to injure the genitals; or if the kick *is* aimed at the genitals, it merely touches them, letting the opponent know that the attacker could have exploded them had he wanted to. The defence here is Cut Bamboo with Branches. The defender moves a small step backwards and slices the palm at the attacking leg, using the technique of no defence, direct counter.

The kicking technique employed in the pattern Naughty Monkey Kicks Tree is known as Whirlwind Kick, which appears to be similar to, but is actually different from, the round-house kick in karate and taekwondo. The Whirlwind Kick is executed from the knee, although the turning of the waist to co-ordinate it is important, whereas the roundhouse kick is usually executed from the waist. The striking point is the shin, and it is usually aimed at the opponent's side ribs.

Whirlwind kicks are frequently used by Siamese Boxing fighters, whose kicks are so fast and powerful that blocking them directly with the arms often results in the arms being fractured. So, how should one block a powerful Whirlwind Kick? The answer is, do not block it. Intercept it at its weakest point, ie at the attacker's knee, or better still, 'thread' the kick away as in the pattern Swimming Dragon Plays with Water. This 'threading' technique is executed as follows: lower and slant your body away to let the whirlwind kick pass; as it passes you, move your palm diagonally forward in an arc as if you were pulling a needle with thread, so that with the back of your diagonally forward-moving arm you push the kicking leg away, following its kicking momentum. This pattern illustrates the principle of 'minimum force against maximum strength'.

Felling and Holding Techniques

Before attempting felling techniques, it is necessary to learn how to break a fall and how to roll away from one. Practise the techniques over a cushioned mat, thick carpet or grassy field.

Breaking a fall needs to be taught by a competent instructor; self-instruction often results in injury. The head must not hit the ground, and the palm or elbow must not be used to break a fall; doing so may cause a fractured wrist or arm.

In Shaolin Kung Fu, rolling away is regarded as better than breaking a fall, but the best choice of all, of course, is to counter the felling technique and avoid falling. Hence, although Shaolin students learn to break falls and roll away, just in case, they seldom use them because their counter techniques are effective.

The names of the patterns for the felling and the holding attacks, as well as their defence techniques, are listed below, and their forms are illustrated in *figures 7.6–7.9*.

- Uprooting Tree
- Naughty Monkey Kicks Tree
- White Monkey Fells Tree
- Precious Duck Swims Through Lotus
- Catching with Single Tiger Claw
- Rolling Thunder Cannon Punch
- Hold a Horse Near a Cliff
- Bend a Branch to Pluck Fruit

In Uprooting Tree the attacker places his or her right leg behind the defender's leg, lowers into the Horseriding Stance for solid balance and pushes forward with the right hand at the defender's shoulder, pushing to make the latter fall backwards. The defender lifts up one leg, places it a short step behind and kicks up the other leg in a Whirlwind Kick at the opponent's ribs. This pattern is Naughty Monkey Kicks Tree, which you learned earlier.

In the second technique, the attacker places the right hip close to the defender's buttocks and puts the right arm round the defender's body on the other side, while the left hand holds the defender's left hand. With a twist of the hip and a turn of the hands, he or she throws the defender over the hip, as in *figure 7.7*. To counter this, the defender swiftly moves the left leg a big step backwards and sits firmly in the Horseriding Stance, simultaneously pushing away the attacker's right hand, and strikes out a low right punch in the pattern Precious Duck Swims Through Lotus. This is the same Precious Duck punch you learned earlier.

In the holding attack, the attacker uses a right Tiger Claw to hold the defender's right wrist. The defender makes a circular movement with the right forearm as follows: using the elbow as a pivot, he or she *continuously* turns the right fist slightly downwards, upwards, and finally downwards like a hanging punch. This circular movement releases the attacker's hold on the wrist, as in *figure 7.8*. Moving forward with one leg, the defender uses the left hand to tame or press down the opponent's front arm, and simultaneously hooks a Cannon Punch at the attacker's face.

Uprooting tree

Naughty Monkey

Fig 7.6 Uprooting Tree and Naughty Monkey

(a)
White Monkey

(b)
Precious Duck

Fig 7.7 White Monkey and Precious Duck

(a)

Arm is being held

(b)

Make circular hand movement

(c)

'Hang' down your fist to release hold

(d)

Canon punch to opponent

Fig 7.8 Tiger Claw and Rolling Thunder

Suppose an attacker locks your neck from behind with the bent right elbow in a pattern known as Hold a Horse Near a Cliff, as in *figure 7.9*. First, if you can, lower your chin in between the attacker's arm and your neck, so that the arm does not suffocate you. Then reach for a finger of the attacker's right hand. If he or she clenches the fingers into a close fist, you will have to dig deep into the fist to get hold of a finger or the thumb. Kick your heel backwards onto the attacker's shin to distract him or her, and immediately bend the finger you have grasped and pull the arm out, thus releasing yourself from the neck lock. Still holding the finger, jerk back your elbow sharply to strike the attacker. This counter-pattern is called Bend a Branch to Pluck Fruit.

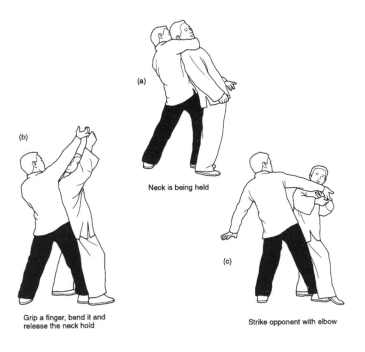

(a)

Neck is being held

(b)

Grip a finger, bend it and
release the neck hold

(c)

Strike opponent with elbow

Fig 7.9 Hold a Horse and Pluck Fruit

As before, first practise the individual patterns until you are familiar with them. Then train on your own, visualizing an imaginary opponent, and later with a partner. Spend about three months practising the techniques against kicks, and another three months on the techniques against felling and holds. Revise the earlier techniques as you practise new ones.

These specific techniques are an effective means of preparing for sparring. They show you what should be done if you are caught in one particular combat situation, but by themselves they are inadequate for fighting, because in a fight your opponent will attack you in a series of aggressive actions, not one action at a time. Even if you know the counters for all the aggressive actions taken individually, you may still be unable to handle them efficiently if they come in a continuous series. In other words, if an opponent gives you a punch, a whirlwind kick, a hip throw or a neck lock one at a time, with a distinct break in between, you can respond effectively. But if these same patterns are executed continuously and fast, you may be overwhelmed, not because you do not know the counters, but because you have not developed the skills to handle a sequence of attacks. We shall learn about these skills in the next chapter.

8

COMBAT SEQUENCES AND SET PRACTICE

What You Must Know Before You Can Fight Well

❖ *Composing your own Kung Fu set will be an interesting and rewarding exercise, even though the resultant set may contain many weaknesses, because you will be experiencing what great masters thought and did.*

Linking Patterns to Form Sequences

The precision and elegance of individual combat techniques shown in martial arts magazines or even in live performances, where one person executes an attack and freezes for the demonstrator to exhibit the pre-arranged response, is meant for demonstration, and does not normally happen in free sparring or a real fight. An opponent in real life does not stop after each attack to wait for your reaction; he or she may shower you with a rain of attacks before you can recover from your first movement.

That does not mean that your free sparring or real fighting cannot be precise and elegant; it can if you are trained. If you are not properly trained, you are unlikely to bring out your best in combat, even though you may execute individual attack and defence patterns beautifully. Thus in free sparring, we often see students merely moving forwards and back-wards, and exchanging blows, instead of applying the beautiful attack and defence patterns which they have learned in their set routines or specific technique training. The reason is that they have not learned the methods and developed the skills for free sparring.

Training in specific techniques, which we looked at in the previous chapter, supplies both the fundamental methods and the skills upon which free sparring is built. Two further stages, with substages, are necessary before we arrive at the point where we are free sparring competently:

combat sequences, which we shall study in this chapter, and combination sets, which will be described in Chapter 10.

A combat sequence is a short series of attack and defence patterns. If you execute Black Tiger Steals Heart by itself, we call it a pattern. If you use it to strike someone, it is a specific technique. In this case it is specifically used to attack your opponent's heart. Your opponent can respond in numerous ways to this particular combat situation; one way which we learned in the previous chapter is Single Tiger Emerges from Cave, which is in this case a specific technique to counter the Black Tiger attack. If you continue from your Black Tiger attack, either before or after your opponent's response, leading to an exchange of attack and defence patterns, this becomes a combat sequence.

A combat sequence can be free, ie you and your training partner can execute patterns according to the demand of each situation. This becomes a short series of free sparring. From their long experience, Shaolin masters discovered that if students were asked to attempt a free combat sequence without adequate preparation, they would be hesitant and indecisive in their exchange. From years of study and experimentation, they devised a series of steps to lead the students from a prearranged to a free combat sequence. In this way the students not only learned attack and defence patterns linked in a logical, advantageous manner, but also developed important skills useful in such combat.

Let us study some ways in which patterns are linked together to form sequences, and the skills that are essential for their effective application. Obviously your chance of defeating your opponent is greater if you use two consecutive attacks instead of one. Your chance is further increased if, instead of deciding what second attack to use only after you have implemented your first attack, you have both ready as soon as you move in to your opponent. For example, as soon as you implement your Black Tiger punch to the heart, you implement the second Precious Duck punch to the abdomen, irrespective of whether your opponent defends effectively against your first attack, and irrespective of what form that defence takes. Opponents who fail to defend against the first attack, will be hit twice; those who succeed with the first defence will be hit in the second attack before they can recover.

You can increase the number to three consecutive attacks. For example, you may start with Poisonous Snake to the throat, then Precious Duck to the abdomen, followed by Black Tiger to the heart. You need not confine yourself to hand attacks; you may introduce kicks, felling techniques or holds at appropriate times. You can have even more consecutive attacks but it is not advisable to do so unless you are specially trained for this kind of attack, because it is easy to fall into the danger of concentrating so hard on attack that defence is neglected.

Even if you use only two consecutive attacking patterns, it is possible that your opponent will counter-attack after your first pattern. Indeed, he or she may surprise you by attacking you first as you move in, even before you have executed your first attack. So you must be prepared for counter-attacks at any time.

Theoretically there are countless ways to counter an attack, and countless ways to continue from an attack or defence pattern. But in practice, the range of responses and of subsequent patterns can usually be narrowed down to a dozen favourite moves, because these give certain technical advantages. For example, if you land a Black Tiger punch, unless your opponent is a master capable of responding in some outlandish way, it is most likely that he or she will either block or dodge your attack. Again there are countless ways of blocking in theory, but in practice the block will usually fall within a range of some preferred patterns. Similarly there is a range of preferred patterns for dodging. Hence, a master with wide experience and understanding will devise combat sequences that will take advantage of these expected movements.

This ability is beyond most students, who are also at a lost when faced with all the possible variations of patterns and sequences. Hence, instead of leaving students in the lurch, masters have chosen appropriate patterns and arranged them in suitable sequences for students to practise. Gradually, as they progress, the control of prearranged patterns and sequences is reduced until eventually they spar freely.

Various Sequences for Practice

If we leave aside defence patterns for the time being, and use X and Y to indicate the attack patterns of the two participants, we may represent some useful sequences for practice as follows:

1 X X
2 X Y X
3 X Y X Y X Y
4 X Y X X Y X X
5 X X X

Suppose that in the combat sequence training, you assume the role of X, and your partner Y. In the sequence X X, you attack twice consecutively and your partner defends accordingly. In X Y X you intend to execute two consecutive attacks, but before you can start the second attack, your partner counter-attacks; thus you defend against his counter-attack and then carry on with your planned second attack. You should have no difficulty working out the meaning of the other sequences.

The following are some examples for your training, starting with simple patterns and proceeding to more complex ones, and using the patterns you learned in Chapter 6. You can use either the left or the right mode of the patterns, whichever is best or most convenient. Practise each sequence at least 10 times per training session, then reverse roles and practise another 10 times.

As the patterns are prearranged, you should focus on developing skills like anticipation, judgement and decisiveness. Later, devise your own patterns according to the suggested sequences above, and then devise your own sequences. Initially do not try to perform the sequences fast, for this may distract you from correctness of form and good balance. As you practise the sequences over and over again, speed will be gradually developed.

Start and complete each combat sequence with any suitable poise patterns, like Lohan Asks the Way or Single Tiger Emerges from Cave (see Chapter 6). If a training partner is not available, use an imaginary opponent.

Sequence 1 – X Y X. Move in to your partner, simultaneously opening or taming his or her hand, and execute Black Tiger Steals Heart. Your opponent responds with Single Tiger Emerges from Cave and immediately counters with Black Tiger Steals Heart. You respond with Single Tiger Emerges from Cave, and then Poisonous Snake Shoots Venom. Your partner defends with Beauty Looks at Mirror.

(a)

(b)

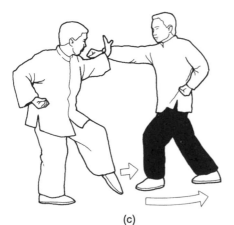

(c)

(d)

Fig 8.1 Combat Sequence 1

Sequence 2 – X Y X.   You attack with Black Tiger and your partner responds with Single Tiger, then Poisonous Snake. You respond with Beauty Looks at Mirror, then Naughty Monkey Kicks Tree. Your partner responds with Swimming Dragon Plays with Water.

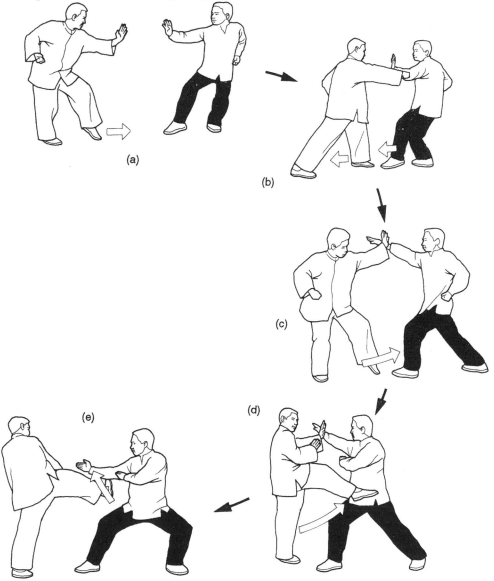

Fig 8.2 Combat Sequence 2

Sequence 3 – X Y X Y X Y.   You attack with Poisonous Snake, and your partner responds with Beauty Looks at Mirror, followed by Precious Duck Swims Through Lotus. You reply with False-Leg Hand Sweep, then Happy Bird Hops up Branch. Your partner attempts to strike your leg with Lohan Strikes Drum, followed by Poisonous Snake. You counter with Beauty Looks at Mirror, then Naughty Monkey Kicks Tree. Your partner respond with Swimming Dragon.

Fig 8.3 Combat Sequence 3

Sequence 4 – X Y X X Y X X. You attack with Golden Star at Corner, to which your partner replies with Immortal Emerges from Cave, followed by Yellow Oriole Drinks Water. You counter with Cut Bamboo with Branches, and Poisonous Snake. As soon as your partner defends with a Mirror Hand, you move forward swiftly and apply Uprooting Tree to fell him or her. Your partner responds with Naughty Monkey, which is a defence and counter pattern. You respond with Tame Tiger with Beads, then move in with Precious Duck. Your partner lowers his or her kicking leg to the back, and simultaneously holds the wrist of your attacking arm. You reply with Rolling Thunder Cannon Punch, which is a defence and counter pattern. As your partner moves back with Single Tiger Emerges from Cave, you continue with Yellow Oriole. Your partner defends with False-Leg Hand Sweep.

Fig 8.4 Combat Sequence 4

Sequence 5 – X X X.   You attack with Poisonous Snake, to which your partner responds with Beauty Looks at Mirror. You immediately follow up with Yellow Oriole. As soon as your partner defends with either False-Leg Hand Sweep or Cut Bamboo with Branches, you kick him or her with your other leg in the Happy Bird Hops up Branch pattern. Your partner quickly retreats a small step to the sideways Bow-Arrow Stance and counters with Lohan Strikes Drum.

Fig 8.5 Combat Sequence 5

When you are familiar with a combat sequence, you can change or add one or two patterns. Gradually this changing or adding of patterns is increased until eventually you are free sparring. If you want to be proficient in your sparring or fighting, you must spend time and effort in combat sequence training. You should practise this course of combat sequences, including your own modifications and compositions, for at least six months.

Relieving Injuries Sustained in Sparring

Despite taking great care not to hurt one another in sparring practice, students are sometimes injured by unintentional hits. When the injury is external, such as a bruise or a swelling, applying some Kung Fu medicine like the medicinal wine described in Chapter 11 can relieve the problem.

If it is internal, such as pain in the chest or abdomen, taking a herbal concoction can overcome the problem. The Harmonizing Chi and Generating Blood concoction is effective for curing internal injuries of a traumatic nature. Its ingredients, named in Chinese, are as follows: *su geng, su mu, hou bu, sa ren, gui wei, mu xiang, chuan hong hua, zhi ke, chi yao, tao ren, xiang fu*. Obtain 8g of each ingredient, and slowly brew the mixture in an earthen pot with three bowls of water. When about a bowl of the mixture remains, pour it from the pot into a bowl, and drink it when it is luke warm. The ingredients may be brewed again the next day, and the mixture taken a second time. If the injury is serious, take three doses (ie six times, brewing new ingredients after every second time) with an interval of three days between doses. (Remember that a dose is a bowl full on two successive days, the second being a brewing of the same ingredients.) Do not worry if you feel more pain the day after you have taken the concoction; that is the effect of the medicine clearing internal blockages. If you have not sustained any obvious injury, it is still advisable to take the concoction once a month if you practise sparring.

Another way to relieve injuries is to practise the appropriate Chi Kung exercises, like Lifting the Sky and Self-Manifested Chi Movement, which will be explained in Chapter 14. Such exercises not only relieve both external and internal injuries, but also enhance many aspects of Kung Fu.

Linking Sequences to Form Sets

One helpful way to remember the Kung Fu patterns that you have learned, like the 24 specific techniques which provide the ingredients for your combat sequence training, is to link them into a meaningful set and supply supplementary patterns for such functions as the greeting poise at the beginning and end of the set.

You may link the patterns in any way you find suitable. The following is one way of joining the eight patterns of hand attack and defence (*see* Chapter 6) into a short set in a simple, but elegant and systematic manner.

Start at a ready position. Move your right leg slightly forward, then your left leg in front of your right leg to form a left False-Leg Stance.

Simultaneously place your left palm and right fist together in front of your chest in the typical Shaolin greeting. This pattern is called Dragon and Tiger Appear. Then retrace your steps and move back to the ready position.

Move your right leg slightly backwards to form a left False-Leg Stance, and simultaneously hold your left palm in front, with elbow slightly bent,

Fig 8.6 Set of hand patterns (Section 1)

while your right fist is still at your right waist. This is a poise pattern, called Lohan Asks the Way. Breathe out gently.

Move your left leg forwards into a left Bow-Arrow Stance, simultaneously taking a quick, deep breath, then punch out your level right fist powerfully with an explosive 'her-it' sound coming from your abdomen. This is the pattern Black Tiger Steals Heart. Pull back your left leg slightly to form a left False-Leg Stance, and move your left Tiger Claw in an arc to the front in the pattern Single Tiger Emerges from Cave, simultaneously making a tiger-like 'yaa...' sound vibrating from your lungs.

Move the left leg forwards again into a left Bow-Arrow Stance, and shoot out your right snake form, making a sharp 'shss' sound, coming from your kidneys, while your left palm is held near your right breast. This pattern is Poisonous Snake Shoots Venom. Without moving your feet, block with your left hand in the pattern Beauty Looks at Mirror, with your right palm near your left elbow. Then gently breathe in.

Bring your back right leg a big step forwards so that it now becomes your front leg, and sit low on a sideways Horseriding Stance. Simultaneously punch out your level right fist in the pattern Precious Duck Swims Through Lotus, with an explosive 'her-it' sound. Then bring your right leg a small step backwards to form a right False-Leg Stance, breathing in at the same time, and sweep your right palm diagonally downwards in the pattern False-Leg Hand Sweep, simultaneously breathing out.

Move the right leg forwards into a right Bow-Arrow Stance, and simultaneously hook out your left Horn Punch, with your right palm guarding your exposed left ribs, in the pattern Golden Star at Corner. Float your right palm towards your upper right, and bring your left fist back to the left of your waist, in the pattern Immortal Emerges from Cave.

These eight basic patterns comprise the first section of the short set as shown in *figure 8.6*.

Figure 8.7 illustrates the second section, which is the same as the first, except that left and right are reversed. Move your right front leg a small step in front and drag your left back leg accordingly a small step forward to remain at a right Bow-Arrow Stance. Simultaneously punch out your level left fist in the Black Tiger pattern, with an explosive 'her-it' sound coming from the abdomen. Take back your right leg into a right False-Leg Stance, and move out your right Tiger Claw with a 'yaaa...' sound.

Continue with Poisonous Snake and Mirror Hand, then move your back left leg a large step forward and execute the Precious Duck punch, followed by False-Leg Hand Sweep. Move a small step forwards to a left Bow–Arrow Stance, and execute a right Horn Punch, followed by Immortal Emerges from Cave with your left hand. Complete this second section with a right Black Tiger Steals Heart, with an explosive 'her-it'

Fig 8.7 Set of hand patterns (Section 2)

sound coming from your abdomen. The Black Tiger punch here is a connecting pattern, added to make the second section connect smoothly with the third.

The third and the fourth sections are the same as the first two except that they are performed in opposite directions, and left and right are reversed. *Figure 8.8* shows the third section. After the *right* Black Tiger punch at a left Bow-Arrow Stance in the last pattern of the second section, without moving the legs make a right about turn to form a right Bow-Arrow Stance and strike out your *left* Black Tiger punch. Move your

Fig 8.8 Set of hand patterns (Section 3)

right leg back slightly to stand at a right False-Leg Stance and execute Single Tiger Emerges from Cave.

Continue with left Poisonous Snake and right Mirror Hand. Then move your left leg a big step forward for the left Precious Duck punch, followed by a left Hand Sweep standing at a left False-Leg Stance. Move forwards with a right Horn Punch, followed by Immortal Emerges from Cave. This completes the third section.

The fourth section is similar to the third except that the left and right modes are reversed, as shown in *figure 8.9*. Without moving your feet, execute a right Black Tiger punch, followed by a left Tiger Claw in Single Tiger Emerges from Cave. Next, shoot out your right snake hand, followed by a left Mirror Hand. Move your right leg a big step forward to execute the right Precious Duck punch, then a right Hand Sweep. Move to a right Bow-Arrow Stance to execute a left Horn Punch, followed by a right Immortal Emerges from Cave. Complete this fourth section with a left Black Tiger punch, which is an additional pattern.

Without moving your legs, make a *left* about turn, and punch out a right Black Tiger Steals Heart, which is an additional pattern. Remaining in this position, change from a left Bow-Arrow Stance to a Horseriding Stance, with your body facing right, your face looking in front at right angles to your body, and your straight left arm extending forward with the One-Finger Zen hand form, and making a 'shss...' sound. Gently sink your Chi, or vital energy, down to your abdominal *dan tian*, and remain in this poise for a few seconds. This pattern is called Stabilizing Cosmos with One-Finger Zen. The One-Finger Zen hand form is a typical Shaolin symbol, and the pattern is sometimes used by masters as a poise pattern, although beginners will find that remaining in a Horseriding Stance is too grounded for fighting.

Change to a left False-Leg Stance with the Shaolin greeting in the pattern Dragon and Tiger Appear. Step back into a ready position to complete this set. For the sake of reference we may call this set Shaolin Hand Attacks.

Composing Your Own Kung Fu Sets

You may arrange these eight basic patterns in any other way you like to compose your own set, and choose your own name for it. You should try arranging the basic patterns for kicks and for falls and holds into suitable sets. You can have one set for one category of attack, as we have done for hand attacks, or a mixture of categories in the same set. You may, if you

Fig 8.9 Set of hand patterns (Section 4)

like, use the Shaolin Hand Attacks as the basis and add patterns for kicks, felling techniques and holds at appropriate places.

Composing your own Kung Fu set will be an interesting and rewarding exercise, even though the resultant set may contain many weaknesses, because you will be experiencing what great masters thought and did with the classical Kung Fu sets which have now become our inheritance.

In the Shaolin Hand Attacks, the movements are forwards and then backwards in one line. This linear arrangement is suitable because the set is short and its patterns are simple. But if your set is long and the patterns varied, you can try other arrangements, such as moving in four directions, in circles, or in asymmetrical designs.

Practising a set gives us other, more important, benefits than just enabling us to remember some patterns. The Shaolin Hand Attack set, for example, helps us to learn breath control, see the relationships in logical sequences, and develop stamina, speed and fluid movement. Whenever you perform the set, you practise all the basic hand patterns four times, which is not only more time-efficient than practising the same patterns separately four times, but also enables you to practise their connecting movements, which will be helpful in combat, when an opponent is likely to attack you not in staccato patterns but in a continuous sequence. You may initially use one breath for each pattern, but as you develop better breath control you may perform a whole section of eight patterns in only one breath, which means not only that your stamina is better, but also that your movements are faster and smoother.

You should spend at least six months on elementary set practice, with Shaolin Hand Attacks and other short, simple sets you may compose. Since practising a set takes only a few minutes, you can follow other courses at the same time. For example, during the six months that you have allotted to developing the skills and techniques associated with set practice, you can also develop other aspects of Kung Fu, like combat application and specific force training, which will be explained later.

Set practice is a basic aspect of Kung Fu training, but unfortunately many students think it is all that Kung Fu represents. Not surprisingly, such students achieve little, even though they may spend many years on Kung Fu. To avoid this mistake, you should define the course and personal objectives for your set practice, as well for other training courses in future.

When you are proficient in simple sets, you may proceed to more complex ones like Shaolin Five Animals, which will be described in the next chapter.

9

SHAOLIN FIVE ANIMALS

Training of Mind, Energy, Essence, Speed and Elegance

❖ *These five animals, therefore, provide Shaolin Kung Fu with their respective characteristics and essence, not only making it an effective fighting art but also enabling it to become an excellent system for physical, emotional, mental and spiritual development.*

Understanding Characteristics and Essence

Many of the extensive patterns in Shaolin Kung Fu are derived from observing the characteristics and essence of animals that surpass those of humans. The agility of the monkey and the stability of the elephant, for example, are qualities that can benefit both martial artists and ordinary people.

Of the numerous animals that have provided inspiration and valuable lessons to Shaolin Kung Fu, the following five are especially significant: dragon, snake, tiger, leopard and crane. Shaolin masters have adopted from these animals not only their outward characteristics, like the Dragon Palm and the Tiger Claw which are incorporated into Kung Fu patterns, but also their inner essence, like the speed of the leopard and the elegance of the crane which have enriched many aspects of Kung Fu training. Each of the five Shaolin animals is noted for its special characteristic and essence.

In Chinese culture, the dragon is a majestic, divine creature which brings luck and prosperity. Its characteristic powerful, undulating and flowing movements are manifested as a graceful, sinuous body motion in Shaolin Kung Fu. If you punch or kick an exponent who specializes in the dragon style, for example, he or she would not block your attack nor move away, but gracefully swerve the body without moving the feet, so that your attack would miss, while he or she would continue the swerving momentum to strike you. The pattern Swimming Dragon Plays with Water, which we learned in the last chapter, is an example of this swerving technique.

In terms of its inner essence, the dragon form is for training *shen*, which means 'mind' or 'spirit'. Stabilizing Cosmos with One-Finger Zen is an example of the dragon form for developing the mind, which means, among other things, that the exponent is peaceful, tranquil and mentally fresh, ready to mobilize every part of the body in a split second. The development of *shen* is often reflected in the sparkle of the master's eye, and in an invisible but discernible force that he radiates.

In some ways the snake resembles a dragon, but without the latter's grandeur and power. It is sometimes called an earthly dragon. Its movement is fast and sleek, its attack vicious, and its most notable characteristic is softness. Hence, a snake form specialist would normally not block an attack directly with physical strength, but would absorb it using circular movements, coil round it, and slide along the attacking limb to strike the opponent's weak spots.

The essence of the snake form is chi or intrinsic energy. The soft, gentle movements of snake patterns are meant to facilitate Chi flow, which can give the exponent tremendous internal force. Such a person does not need external force training like hitting sandbags and striking poles, which are actually incongruous to the snake form.

The tiger is well known for its ferocity and power. It may surprise those who have not observed a tiger closely, to know that its movements are also very agile and elegant. Thus, if you perform tiger patterns like Black Tiger Steals Heart and Single Tiger Emerges from Cave clumsily or without power, you will miss the characteristics that are meant to be expressed in these patterns.

The power of the tiger form is not mechanical or brutal. In Kung Fu terminology, the essence of the tiger lies in its bones, which is a figurative way of saying that the training of the tiger form is to develop internal force. The internal force used in the tiger form training is different from that of the snake. The tiger form emphasizes *jing*, or 'essence', which is matter in its finest form, similar to what modern scientists call subatomic particles. The snake form emphasizes chi, or intrinsic energy. *Jing* and chi are nevertheless relative; *jing* can be converted to chi, and vice versa. It is amazing that Shaolin masters preceded modern scientists in this concept of the relativity of matter and energy by many centuries.

The characteristic of the leopard is speed; leopard patterns are therefore fast. In Shaolin Kung Fu the leopard form is represented by the Leopard Punch, which is formed by bending the knuckles at the second finger joints, and not at the third, as in a normal fist. However, if you perform the Black Tiger punch or the Happy Bird side kick at great speed, your pattern has the characteristic of the leopard, even though it is named after a tiger or a bird. Hence, it is often the characteristic, and not just the form, of a pattern that counts.

The essence of the leopard lies in its muscles, which means that in the leopard form, the emphasis is on external strength. Unlike internal force, which can be inflicted at the point of contact, external strength depends to a great extent on fast movement for its successful operation. If your Dragon Palm is on your opponent's chest, for example, you can cause a lot of injury if you exert internal force, without having to pull it back some distance to ram it in. But if you use a Leopard Punch, you have to drive it into your opponent with speed and momentum.

Why, then, is the leopard form, with its external strength, not replaced by the tiger, which emphasizes internal force? It is because, among other reasons, the leopard form has the advantage of speed, which also complements its external strength. The tiger techniques are generally not as speedy, unless they are generated by internal chi flow, which can make them very fast. Many other martial arts actually depend mainly on speed and external strength – the characteristic and essence of the leopard.

If you observe a crane, you will probably be impressed by its stability and tranquillity, and perhaps be surprised that its slender solitary-standing leg can support such an enormous weight. The bird seems to be frozen in space and time. When it suddenly takes off, despite its huge size and apparent immobility, its movements are swift and graceful, demonstrating an excellent way of both conserving and using energy. Manifested in Shaolin Kung Fu, the characteristic of the crane form is elegance, and its essence is quiescence.

While patterns involving standing on one leg as in kicking, spreading the arms like the crane's wings and using the crane beak are discernible expressions of the crane form, other patterns which demonstrate elegance or quiescence also derive their inspiration from the crane. Most patterns named after birds are included in the general category of the crane form. Oriole Drinks Water, despite its name, is an exquisite crane technique, executing a kick unobtrusively but efficaciously. On the other hand, elaborated and exposed high kicks, especially those accompanied by a lot of shouting as if warning the opponent that the kicks are coming, are not representative of the crane, because, from the Shaolin perspective, they lack elegance and quiescence, which in Kung Fu terms means that they are not only clumsy and unsightly to watch, but also technically inferior and wasteful of energy.

These five animals, therefore, provide Shaolin Kung Fu with their respective characteristics and essence, not only making it an effective fighting art but also enabling it to become an excellent system for physical, emotional, mental and spiritual development. The form and significance of the tiger, snake and dragon develop what are called the three treasures, namely *jing*, chi and *shen*, which are matter in its finest form (or subatomic particles), intrinsic energy, and mind or spirit. A person whose *jing* is full, for example, is physically fit and healthy; one whose chi is plentiful is emotionally stable and full of vitality; and one whose *shen* is abundant is mentally fresh and spiritually mature.

The leopard form and significance produce speed and agility, while those of the crane produce elegance and tranquillity. How and why Shaolin Kung Fu leads to emotional growth, mind expansion and spiritual development will be explained in later chapters.

Some Preliminary Information

Figures 9.1–9.9 show the patterns of the set called the Shaolin Five-Animal set, and the description in the next section explains the main points. I composed this set specially for this book, drawing inspiration and material from some of the best classical Shaolin Kung Fu patterns.

As I said, it is difficult to learn Kung Fu movements from a book, so you should ideally seek an instructor. But if this is not feasible, try to follow the pictures and description as best as you can, without worrying unduly about details. If you are still not clear about the various Shaolin hand forms and stances, you should read Chapter 6 again, because they will be mentioned extensively.

Practise the patterns slowly and leisurely at first, paying careful attention to performing the form correctly. Then practise each pattern with force, gradually developing your force pattern by pattern, but remember that your force must be flowing, not locked in your chest, shoulders or elbows. If your force, or more likely your brute strength, is locked, you will feel crammed or painful after sustained practice. If your force is flowing, you will feel fresh and energized.

When you can perform the whole set with accurate form and flowing force, progress to practising with speed. An important factor in speed training is not just performing each pattern faster, but flowing from one pattern to another smoothly. You should be performing continuous sequences of numerous patterns, and not each pattern individually. This development of accurate form, force and speed should be progressive and gradual, so you may not feel much difference between two consecutive days in your training. But there will be a tremendous difference between the first and the last days of the period you set for this training course, which should be about six months. Remember to work out your personal and course objectives, and evaluate them at the end of the course.

The most important aspect is that you must express the characteristics and essence of the five Shaolin animals as you perform their respective patterns. When you are performing a dragon pattern, for example, you should develop mind control to channel internal force to wherever it is wanted; when you are performing a tiger pattern, you should feel the courage and power of a tiger, and not perform it as if you were a cat. You will have a better understanding of mind control and internal force after you have read some of the later chapters.

The Five-Animal Set

1 **Dragon and Tiger Appear.**   Start from the ready position; move to Dragon and Tiger Appear (*see* pages 94–5) and pose for a few seconds, with your chi gently focused at the abdomen; then return to the ready position. Dragon and Tiger Appear is a Shaolin greeting pattern, usually performed at the start and end of a Kung Fu set. It is also frequently used to greet a partner in a training session, or an opponent before a real combat; Shaolin disciples should not be impolite even in a fight. When it is used as a greeting to a partner or an opponent, it is often performed while standing upright, and not in the False-Leg Stance.

2 **Single Dragon Emerges from Sea (right).**   Move to the Horseriding Stance. Hold your right hand in the dragon form; move out and bring back the dragon form three times. Breathe in gently through your nose as you draw your dragon form in, and breathe out gently through your mouth with a 'Shsss...' sound as you move it out, using your mind power to direct vital energy from your abdomen to your fingertips. After moving your dragon form out and drawing it in three times, 'shoot' it out with a 'her-it' sound. Then bring your right hand in a fist back to your waist.

3 **Single Dragon Emerges from Sea (left).**   Repeat pattern 2 above, substituting right for left. As it is a dragon pattern, its aim is to train *shen* or mind. Correct training enables you to use your mind to channel internal power to your fingers. Apart from your hand or fingers, which are charged with energy, you should be totally relaxed.

4 Swimming Dragon Plays with Water (right). Imagine that you have performed patterns 1, 2 and 3 facing north. Now move your right leg to north-east, by first transferring your body weight onto your left leg, swerving in an anticlockwise circular movement to your back and then to your front, and then transferring your weight evenly over both legs. Your body should lean slightly forward after the circular swerving movement, but without affecting your balance. Simultaneously thread (see Chapter 7, p.79) your right palm forward, with your left palm near your right elbow.

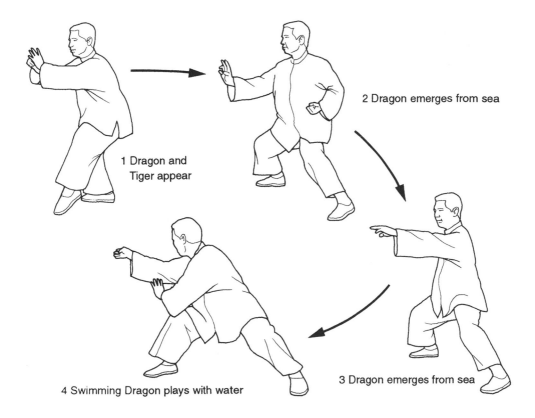

1 Dragon and Tiger appear

2 Dragon emerges from sea

3 Dragon emerges from sea

4 Swimming Dragon plays with water

Fig 9.1 The Five-Animal set, patterns 1–4

5 **Swimming Dragon Plays with Water (left).**   Repeat pattern 4, substituting right for left, and moving towards the north-west. The significant feature of these two patterns is the flowing circular body movement, and the threading technique. Train your mind to direct your vital energy to flow with your movement.

6 **Green Dragon Shoots out Pearl.**   Circle your left palm in an anticlockwise direction in front, and simultaneously strike out your right palm. Let your internal force shoot out from your palm.

7 **Poisonous Snake Basks in Mist.**   Bring back your left leg to form a left False-Leg Stance facing north, and simultaneously bring both hands in snake forms in a circular movement to your chest level, with your left palm in front. Breathe in into your abdomen.

8 **Poisonous Snake Shoots Venom (left).**   Immediately move forward towards north to a left Bow-Arrow Stance and shoot out your left snake form at your opponent's throat, with your right snake form near your left elbow. Direct chi to your fingertips with a 'shssk' sound.

Fig 9.2 The Five-Animal set, patterns 5–8

9 **Poisonous Snake Shoots Venom (right).** Immediately shoot out your right snake form, and place your left snake form near your right elbow. Direct chi to your fingertips with a 'shssk' sound.

10 **Single Tiger Emerges from Cave.**   Bring your left leg back into a left False-Leg Stance, and move your left Tiger Claw in an arc to your front, with a 'yaa...' sound vibrating from your lungs. Open your eyes wide, and focus your internal power at your Tiger Claw. Feel the courage and power of a tiger.

11 **Black Tiger Steals Heart.**   Move forward into a left Bow-Arrow Stance, and strike out your level right fist with a 'her-it' sound coming from your abdomen. Imagine your punch is so powerful that it fells a wall.

12 **Hungry Tiger Catches Goat.**   Move your right back leg a big step forward to form a right Bow-Arrow Stance, circle your right Tiger Claw in a small anti-clockwise movement, move your left Tiger Claw forward, and lean your body slightly in front, making a 'yaa...' sound. Open your eyes wide and feel the ferocity of a hungry tiger.

Fig 9.3 The Five-Animal set, patterns 9–12

13 **Angry Leopard Charges at Rock.**   Swiftly retreat to a right False-Leg Stance, and jab your right Leopard Punch diagonally downwards.

14 **Golden Leopard Speeds Through Jungle (left).**   Move your right leg forward to a right Bow-Arrow Stance, and strike out your left Leopard Punch, placing your right Leopard Punch near your left elbow. The essence here is speed.

15 **Golden   Leopard   Speeds   Through   Jungle   (right).** Instantaneously strike out your right Leopard Punch, pulling back your left Leopard Punch at your right elbow. The two Leopard Punches are to be performed as if they are one pattern. Patterns 7–15 are performed facing north.

16 **Reincarnated Crane (left).**   Move your left leg diagonally forward so that it is in line with your right leg, and form a right False-Leg Stance with your body slanting slightly backwards. Simultaneously use your right Crane Beak to hook your opponent's arm, and use your left Crane Beak to strike his or her temple. Your stance points east, but your crane strike is towards the north-east. You should perform this pattern elegantly.

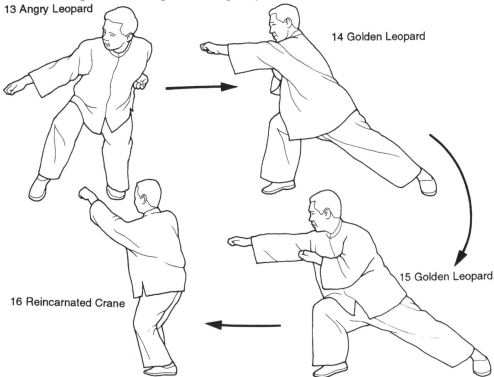

13 Angry Leopard

14 Golden Leopard

15 Golden Leopard

16 Reincarnated Crane

Fig 9.4 The Five-Animal set, patterns 13–16

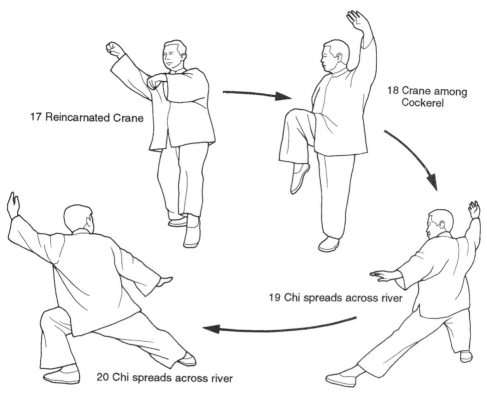

17 Reincarnated Crane

18 Crane among Cockerel

19 Chi spreads across river

20 Chi spreads across river

Fig 9.5 The Five-Animal set, patterns 17–20

17 **Reincarnated Crane (right).** Shift your weight to your right leg, make a left about turn, and repeat pattern 16, reversing left and right. Now your stance points towards west, but your strike is towards north-west. These two crane patterns must be performed elegantly.

18 **Crane Stands Among Cockerels.** Turn to face north, stand in a left Single-Leg Stance, spread out both hands, and kick out your right leg with the instep as the striking point. This is a very elegant pattern. Remain at the tranquil poise for a few seconds.

19 **Dragon's Chi Spreads Across the River (left).** Lower your right leg and place it behind to form a left Front-Arrow Stance, still facing north. Spread out both arms, with your back right palm facing upwards above your head and your front left palm facing downwards near your left knee. Focus your chi at your abdomen, then channel it to flow to your two arms.

20 **Dragon's Chi Spreads Across the River (right).** Shift your body weight to your left front leg and turn around to form a right Front-Arrow Stance, facing south. Spread both arms. Focus at your

abdomen and channel chi to both arms. These two dragon patterns, patterns 19 and 20, which are similar but reversed, are to be performed slowly (except when you are using them in combat), so that you can concentrate your *shen* and chi. You should be mentally fresh, and experience energy flow inside your body.

21 **Fierce Dragon Speeds Across Stream.** First bring your right leg back near to your left in a momentary Cat Step (which is like a False-Leg Stance but with the feet closer together), place your left palm in front and your right palm behind near your right breast, then instantly shoot out your right leg into a right Bow-Arrow Stance and strike out your right palm, with the edge of your palm as striking point. Feel yourself like a stream of energy shooting forwards, but take care that your weight is evenly distributed between both legs, although your body may lean forward slightly.

22 **Black Tiger Speeds Across Valley.** Bring you back left leg near to your front right leg, and immediately shoot out your front leg into a right Bow-Arrow Stance, simultaneously striking out your level right fist. While this pattern is named after the tiger to emphasize the use of internal force rather than brute strength, its speed is characteristic of the leopard.

23 **Fierce Tiger Crouches on Ground.** In patterns 20–22, you faced south. Now turn your body 180 degrees to the left, so that it points north, but you look towards the east. Crouch with your right knee on the ground, place your left Tiger Claw near your shoulder and your right Tiger Claw a short distance in front near the ground. Focus internal force on your right Tiger Claw.

24 **Spiritual Dragon Rises Towards Sky.** Focus your chi at your abdomen, change your Tiger Claws into Dragon Palms and rise up, bringing your left leg diagonally backward into a left sideways Bow-Arrow Stance, simultaneously pushing both palms with some force towards the sky. As you rise, let your chi rise through your body to your arms and palms, while still maintaining a firm stance. In this pattern, if you draw a line from your right leg to your left leg, it will point towards the south-west, but you should looking towards the north-west.

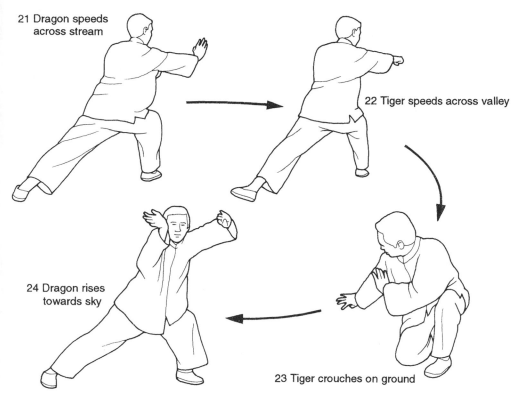

Fig 9.6 The Five-Animal set, patterns 21–24

25 **Double Dragons Play with Pearl.** Without moving your feet, turn left towards the south-west, shift your body backwards to your back right leg, bending your right knee more than your left, and simultaneously lower your hands as if you are holding a ball close to the left side of your body but with both fists clenched. Your left elbow should be close to your waist while your right arm should be at shoulder level. Instantaneously move forward to a left Bow-Arrow Stance, still facing south-west, and strike out both fists, the left lower fist at your opponent's solar plexus, and the right upper fist at the face. Your fists should be held facing each other, ie if the palms were open the left palm would face upward and the right palm downwards.

26 **White Tiger Presents Claw.** Make a right about turn and stand in a right False-Leg Stance, but with the body leaning slightly backwards. Swing your left Tiger Claw from below upwards and forwards. Focus internal force at your left Tiger Claw. Your stance should point north-east, but your Tiger Claw strike should be towards the north where your imaginary opponent is.

27 Fierce Tiger Descends Mountain. Move your right leg forwards to a right Bow-Arrow Stance, with your body leaning forwards but without upsetting your balance, and strike out your right Tiger Claw in a forward and slightly downward movement, with your left Tiger Claw following near the right elbow. Focus internal force at both Tiger Claws. This pattern points towards the north-east.

28 Golden Leopard Watches Fire. Without moving from your position, make a 270 degree left-about turn to face south-east, sit on the ground in a Seven-Star Stance, and strike your left Leopard Punch upwards and backwards. The emphasis is on speed.

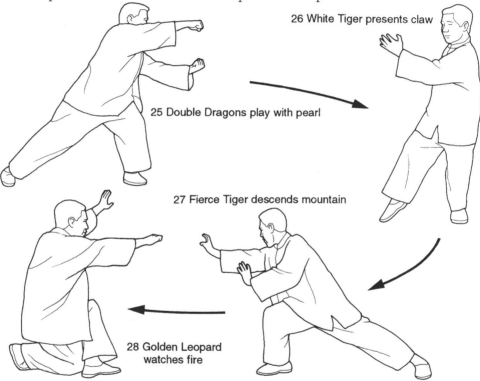

26 White Tiger presents claw

25 Double Dragons play with pearl

27 Fierce Tiger descends mountain

28 Golden Leopard watches fire

Fig 9.7 The Five-Animal set, patterns 25–28

29 Crane Drinks Beside Stream. Immediately move your left leg diagonally forwards into a left sideways Bow-Arrow Stance in a south-easterly direction, with your body leaning forwards, and strike out your right Phoenix-Eye Punch forwards and downwards towards the south-west. Attempt to make the change from patterns 27–28 to this pattern so fast that onlookers do not realize what has happened.

30 **Black Tiger Presents Claw.** Without moving from your leg position, change to a right sideways Bow-Arrow Stance pointing northwest, and strike out your left Tiger Claw towards the west, with your right Tiger Claw a short distance in front of your body.

31 **Old Dragon Takes Water.** Move your left leg forwards to form a left Bow-Arrow Stance pointing west, make a small clockwise circle with your left Dragon Palm in front of your body, and then strike out your right Dragon Palm, pulling back your left palm near to your waist.

32 **White Snake Crosses Valley.** Move your right leg a big step forwards and shift your left leg accordingly so that you now stand at a right Bow-Arrow Stance towards the north, with your body leaning forwards. At the same time stretch both hands in snake form so that your right hand reaches as far forwards, and your left hand as far backwards as possible. Let your chi flow to both hands. From this pattern to the end of the set, your face should be towards the north.

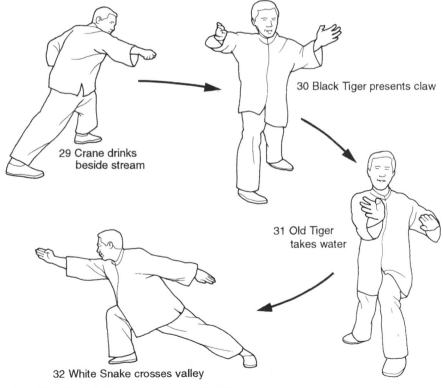

30 Black Tiger presents claw

29 Crane drinks
beside stream

31 Old Tiger
takes water

32 White Snake crosses valley

Fig 9.8 The Five-Animal set, patterns 29–32

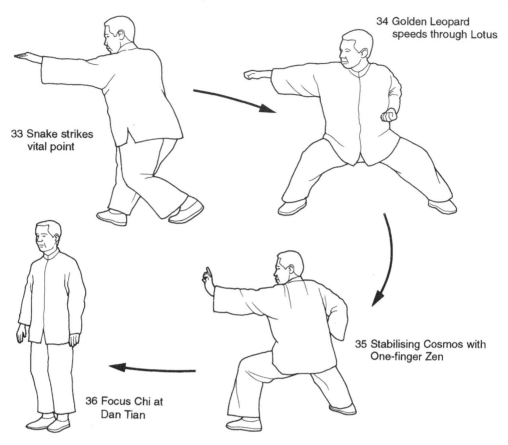

Fig 9.9 The Five-Animal set, patterns 33–36

33 Poisonous Snake Strikes Vital Point. Bring your right leg back and place it a small step in front of your left leg to form a Unicorn Step, and strike out your left snake form.

34 Golden Leopard Speeds Through Lotus. Turn to the left to form a right sideways Horseriding Stance, with your body pointing west, and quickly strike out your right Leopard Punch, with both your face and your strike towards the north.

35 Stabilizing Cosmos with One-Finger Zen. Take your right leg back a big step to form a sideways Horseriding Stance, with your body pointing east, and gradually stretch out your left hand in a One-Finger Zen form, with both your face and your finger still towards the north. Gently sink your chi to your abdominal *dan tian*, and focus your mind on the tip of your finger. Feel calm and alert. Remain at this tranquillity for a few seconds.

36 **Focus Chi at *Dan Tian*.** Turn to perform Dragon and Tiger Unite, which is the same as Dragon and Tiger Appear in pattern 1, gently breathing into your abdomen at the same time. Then return to a ready position, open your fists into palms, gently raise both palms to breast level, turn them to face downwards and gently lower them so that your arms drop naturally to your sides, simultaneously breathing out and visualizing your chi collecting at your abdominal *dan tian*, which is about 3in below your navel. It is very important that the sinking of your chi to your *dan tian* be done gently. With proper practice, you should not feel tired or out of breath after completing this set, even if you have performed it forcefully and speedily; instead, you should feel calm, fresh and energized.

The Names of the Five-Animal Patterns

The names of the 36 patterns of the Five-Animal set are listed below. In Chinese they are poetic and meaningful, although the poetry and meaning are often lost during translation due to the cultural and linguistic differences between Chinese and English.

 1 Dragon and Tiger Appear
 2 Single Dragon Emerges from Sea (right)
 3 Single Dragon Emerges from Sea (left)
 4 Swimming Dragon Plays with Water (right)
 5 Swimming Dragon Plays with Water (left)
 6 Green Dragon Shoots out Pearl
 7 Poisonous Snake Basks in Mist
 8 Poisonous Snake Shoots out Venom (left)
 9 Poisonous Snake Shoots out Venom (right)
10 Single Tiger Emerges from Cave
11 Black Tiger Steals Heart
12 Hungry Tiger Catches Goat
13 Angry Leopard Charges at Rock
14 Golden Leopard Speeds Through Jungle (left)
15 Golden Leopard Speeds Through Jungle (right)
16 Reincarnated Crane (left)
17 Reincarnated Crane (right)
18 Crane Stands Among Cockerels
19 Dragon's Chi Spreads Across River (left)
20 Dragon's Chi Spreads Across River (right)

21 Fierce Dragon Speeds Across Stream
22 Black Tiger Speeds Across Valley
23 Fierce Tiger Crouches on Ground
24 Spiritual Dragon Rises Towards Sky
25 Double Dragons Play with Pearl
26 White Tiger Presents Claw
27 Fierce Tiger Descends Mountain
28 Golden Leopard Watches Fire
29 Crane Drinks Beside Stream
30 Black Tiger Presents Claw
31 Old Dragon Takes Water
32 White Snake Crosses Valley
33 Poisonous Snake Strikes Vital Point
34 Golden Leopard Speeds Through Lotus
35 Stabilizing Cosmos with One-Finger Zen
36 Focus Chi at Dan Tian

People who are uninformed about the intricacies of Shaolin Kung Fu may think that the patterns in this Shaolin Five-Animal set are merely flowery, meant only for demonstrations. Pleasing spectators has never been a function of Shaolin Kung Fu; if Shaolin Kung Fu performances are beautiful to watch – and they are – it is an incidental bonus. Its main aim is self-defence and personal growth. How these Five-Animal patterns can be applied to combat is explained in the next chapter in the form of a combination set.

10

FIVE-ANIMAL COMBINATION SET

Learning to Fight Through Prearranged Sparring

❖ *You should try to develop skills like spacing, timing, balance and fluidity of movement by practising the combination set with a training partner or an imaginary opponent.*

How to Improve Combat Efficiency

As we have seen, some people, including Kung Fu students, believe that if they know Kung Fu sets, they know how to fight. It is like thinking that if you learn the techniques of football or swimming, you can play football or swim. Of course you cannot; you need to practise on the football field or in the swimming pool. Similarly, Kung Fu sets provide useful techniques, but to fight well, you need other ingredients like judgement, quick thinking, speed, power, spacing, timing, balance and fluidity of movement. And most important of all, you need to practise fighting, usually in the form of sparring. If you have never sparred, it is unlikely that you can fight, even if you have practised Kung Fu sets all your life.

Shaolin Kung Fu is rich in ways of developing combat efficiency. Specific techniques, combat sequences, combination sets, force training, and the principles of tactics and strategies are the specialized areas for combat training. Briefly, specific techniques provide you with knowledge and practice in overcoming particular combat situations; combat sequences enable you to apply these techniques in continuous fighting, with training in judgement and quick thinking to meet changing situations in the fight; combination sets allow you to improve your spacing, timing, balance and fluidity of movement; force training supplies the power, speed and agility that are crucial in winning a fight; and the principles of tactics and strategies help you to use your brain as well as your strength to clinch victory.

In this chapter we shall study a combination set based on the Five-Animal set we learned in the last chapter. A combination set is where two or more participants go over a routine of prearranged sparring patterns. It is much longer than a combat sequence, and serves different training purposes, although there are some overlapping factors. An average combat sequence consists of about three to six exchanges, whereas an average combination set consists of between 20 and 30. Because combat sequences are short, participants have more opportunities to develop their judgement and decision making in combat, as they frequently modify or change patterns from the prearranged sequences. Modification or changes are seldom made in combination sets, so that students can better concentrate on their prearranged patterns to improve such skills as spacing, timing, balance and fluid movement.

Hence, in the following combination set of the Five Animals, besides learning the combat application of all the patterns from the Five-Animal set, and how they are linked to achieve certain technical advantages you should try to develop skills like spacing, timing, balance and fluidity of movement, by practising the combination set with a training partner or an imaginary opponent.

The Fascination of Kung Fu Application

For convenience, the two participants in the combination set are referred to as X and Y. The form and movement of the patterns, which are shown in *figures 10.1–10.6*, are not explained in detail in the description, which only mentions the most important points.

1 **Greetings.**   Be prepared for your opponent to attack you while you greet him. If he does, which is of course discourteous, you should just move to an appropriate response, treating your greeting pattern as part of the combat sequence. A useful piece of advice is: be gallant but be always prepared for your opponent to be a rogue. See *figure 10.1 (a)*

2 **Poise patterns.**   X uses a variation of Single Dragon Emerges from Sea as a poise pattern, while Y uses Stabilizing Cosmos with One-Finger Zen, as in *figure 10.1 (b)*. Both are dragon forms, intended to enable the practitioners to be calm and alert.

3 **Golden Leopard Speeds Through Jungle.**   X initiates the combat with a fast attack, driving a right Leopard Punch at Y – *figure 10.1 (c)*.

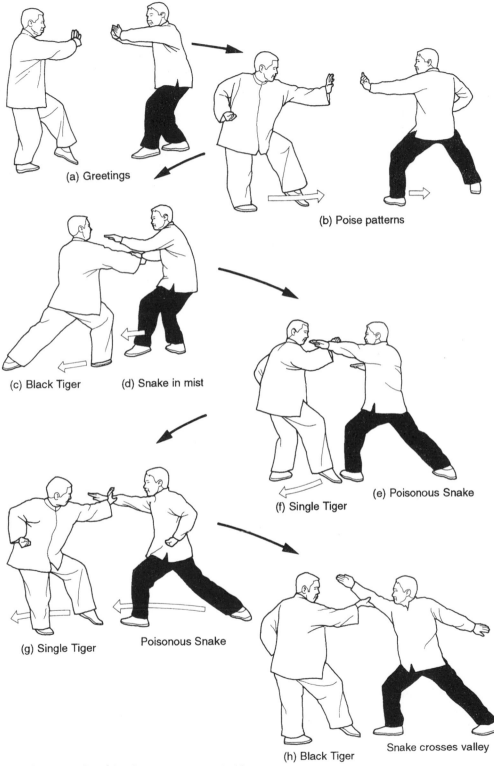

(a) Greetings

(b) Poise patterns

(c) Black Tiger (d) Snake in mist

(e) Poisonous Snake

(f) Single Tiger

(g) Single Tiger Poisonous Snake

(h) Black Tiger Snake crosses valley

Fig 10.1 Combination set, patterns 1–10

4 **Poisonous Snake Basks in Mist.**   Y retreats to a False-Leg Stance, 'shallowing' X's attack, and coils a snake-head on X's forearm, ready to shoot out – *figure 10.1 (c)*.

5 **Poisonous Snake Shoots out Venom (left).**   Y shoots out a left snake form at X's throat, with a right snake form guarding X's arm – *figure 10.1 (d)*.

6 **Single Tiger Emerges from Cave (right).**   X takes the front leg back to a right False-Leg Stance to avoid the snake attack, and uses a right Tiger Claw first to lean on the attacker's forearm, then to grip on the wrist – *figure 10.1 (d)*.

7 **Poisonous Snake Shoots out Venom (right).**   With a circular turn of the wrist, Y avoids X's attempt to grip the left wrist, and simultaneously shoots out a right snake form at X's throat – *figure 10.1 (e)*.

8 **Single Tiger Emerges from Cave (left).**   X retreats to a left False-Leg Stance and uses a left Tiger Claw to grip Y's right wrist – *figure 10.1 (e)*.

9 **White Snake Crosses Valley.**   Y immediately releases the grip by making a circular twist of the right wrist, then moving the right leg forwards, swings up the right hand to slice X's body from the stomach to the chin – *figure 10.1 (f)*.

10 **White Tiger Presents Claw.**   X moves the left leg back to form a right False-Leg Stance to avoid the snake attack, and simultaneously grips Y's elbow with a right Tiger Claw. This is attacking Y at his or her weak point, following the momentum of the attack – *figure 10.1 (f)*.

11 **Poisonous Snake Strikes Vital Point.**   Y circles the right forearm in an anticlockwise movement to push away the Tiger Claw grip, simultaneously changing into a Unicorn Step and using the left snake form to strike a vital point below X's armpit. This is defence and counter – *figure 10.2 (a)*.

12 **Hungry Tiger Catches Goat.**   X uses a right Tiger Claw to tame the snake attack, and simultaneously presses forwards with the right leg to attack Y's face with a left Tiger Claw. This is the formidable Shaolin Double Tiger Claws. See *figure 10.2 (b)*.

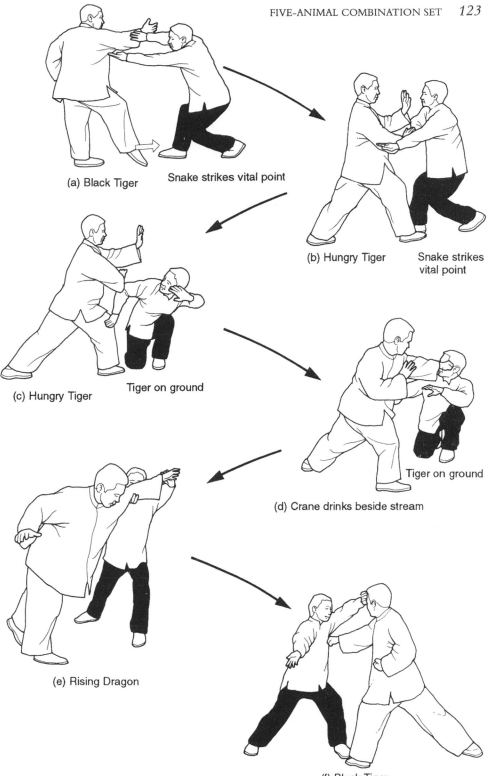

(a) Black Tiger   Snake strikes vital point

(b) Hungry Tiger   Snake strikes
vital point

(c) Hungry Tiger   Tiger on ground

(d) Crane drinks beside stream

Tiger on ground

(e) Rising Dragon

(f) Black Tiger

Fig 10.2 Combination set, patterns 11–16

13 **Fierce Tiger Crouches on Ground.** Instead of meeting the pressing attack of X's Double Tiger Claws, Y crouches on the ground and grips X's ankle with a right Tiger Claw – *figure 10.2 (c)*.

14 **Crane Drinks Beside Stream.** X quickly lifts the leg to avoid the Tiger Claw, moves diagonally forwards, and simultaneously uses a left Phoenix-Eye Punch to strike a vital point at Y's shoulder joint, which controls the muscles holding the forearm to the shoulder – *figure 10.2 (d)*. This strike can immobilize Y's forearm.

15 **Spiritual Dragon Rises Towards Sky.** Y wards off the Phoenix-Eye strike and holds X's elbow with the left hand, supporting X's body with the shoulder, and holds X's leg with the right hand. With the help of the body's rising momentum, he or she throws X off the ground – *figure 10.2 (e)*.

16 **Black Tiger Steals Heart.** With a clockwise circular sweep of the left hand to push off the elbow hold, and jumping diagonally forward with the left and then immediately the right leg, X avoids Y's throw. X instantly makes a left about turn and drives a straight punch into Y – *figure 10.2 (f)*.

17 **Green Dragon Shoots out Pearl.** With a clockwise circular movement of the left hand, Y sweeps away X's punch, and simultaneously strikes X's chest with a right Dragon Palm. This is defence and counter. See *figure 10.3 (a)*.

18 **Fierce Tiger Descends Mountain.** X moves the back right leg diagonally to the right, then brings the left leg close to the right leg in a left Cat Step – *figure 10.3 (b)* – then immediately moves the left leg forward and attacks Y's head with a left Tiger Claw, while a right Tiger Claw guards Y's left hand – *figure 10.3 (c)*.

19 **Golden Leopard Watches Fire.** Y sits on the ground in the Seven-Star Stance, turns the body to the left and strikes X's ribs with a Leopard Punch in a beautiful no defence, direct counter – *figure 10.3 (d)*.

20 **Crane Drinks Beside Stream.** X moves the front left leg diagonally forwards, thus avoiding Y's attack, and simultaneously strikes Y's temple with a right Phoenix-Eye Punch in another beautiful no-defence, direct counter – *figure 10.3 (e)*.

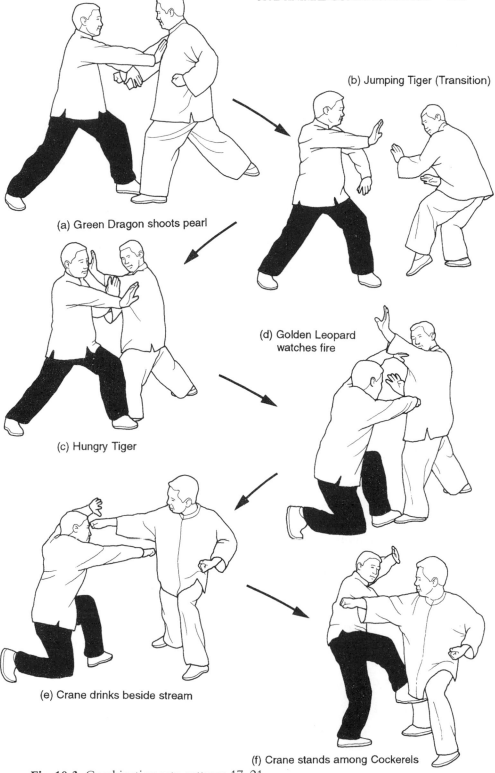

(a) Green Dragon shoots pearl

(b) Jumping Tiger (Transition)

(c) Hungry Tiger

(d) Golden Leopard watches fire

(e) Crane drinks beside stream

(f) Crane stands among Cockerels

Fig 10.3 Combination sets, patterns 17–21

21 **Crane Stands Among Cockerels.** Y springs up to the left and kicks X's genitals with the right leg in what is called the Organ-Seeking Kick – *figure 10.3 (f)*. In line with the compassionate teachings of Shaolin, Y would just touch the opponent's organ, instead of exploding it as a hard kick could.

Spacing and Timing in Combat

22 **Swimming Dragon Plays with Water.** X moves the right back leg a small step further backwards, swerves to avoid Y's kick, and uses the left hand to thread the kicking leg away – *figure 10.4 (a)*.

23 **Golden Leopard Speeds Through Jungle.** Immediately X moves the left front leg a step forwards and strikes with a right Leopard Punch at Y's soft spot below the ribs – *figure 10.4 (b)*.

24 **Black Tiger Presents Claw.** Y places the right leg behind, thus moving the body backwards to avoid the Leopard Punch, sits in a sideways Bow-Arrow Stance and grips X's wrist with a right Tiger Claw, and X's vital point below the armpit with a left Tiger Claw – *figure 10.4 (c)*.

25 **Poisonous Snake Basks in Mist.** Before Y can successfully apply the Tiger Claw grip, X quickly sits back on the right back leg in a left False-Leg Stance, sharply jerks the right hand downwards against Y's wrist, and lowers the forearm close to the body to protect the armpit – all in the same smooth movement, thus neutralizing Y's attack. X is about to shoot out a snake pattern, but Y swiftly moves away into a poise pattern, Swimming Dragon Plays with Water – *figure 10.4 (d)*.

26 **Swimming Dragon Plays with Water.** Y's Swimming Dragon Plays with Water is a very good poise pattern, as it is well covered for defence, as well as ready for instant attack. X remains with Poisonous Snake Basks in Mist, which is another excellent poise pattern, as it also provides good defence coverage and attack readiness, although it is different from Swimming Dragon in many ways. Both combatants assess each other for opportunities.

27 **Dragon's Chi Spreads Across River.** As both poise patterns constitute very good defence positions, neither combatant wishes to attack. Among masters, the one who starts an attack is at a slight disadvantage, unless there is a good opportunity. Thus X changes from

(a) Swimming Dragon

(b) Golden Leopard

(c) Black tiger presents claw

(d)   Snake basks in mist

(e)   Poise patterns

Fig 10.4 Combination set, patterns 22–27

the Poisonous Snake Basks in Mist poise pattern to a variation of Dragon's Chi Spreads Across the River to offer Y an opening – *figure 10.4 (e)*. As this poise pattern is wide open, it is not suitable for beginners; but you must be very careful if a master uses it, for he is likely to employ it as a bait.

28 **Black Tiger Crosses Valley.**   Y moves in with a right Bow-Arrow Stance and a straight right punch. This is an appropriate attack against an open poise pattern which may be a bait, because this attack, in a straight line, minimizes the areas which the opponent can exploit – *figure 10.5 (a)*. Moreover, as this tiger form uses internal force and not external strength, it is not necessary to use charging momentum, which means Y can move in cautiously, thus eliminating the risk involved in rushing in.

29 **Crane Stands Among Cockerels.**   As Y's punch approaches, X shifts his or her body weight to the left leg and inflicts a right snap kick to Y's ribs. This is no defence, direct counter, which is an advanced way of countering. See *figure 10.5 (a)*.

30 **Poisonous Snake Strikes Vital Point.**   Y turns to a Unicorn Step, thus avoiding X's kick. The right hand guards against any further variation of the kicking leg. Simultaneously a left snake form strikes a vital point below X's breast – *figure 10.5 (b)*.

31 **Crane Drinks Beside Stream.**   X brings the right leg back immediately after the kick, uses the right palm to push aside Y's arm, then moves the right leg diagonally forwards, and simultaneously uses a left Phoenix-Eye Punch to strike Y's vital point at the waist – *figure 10.5 (c)*.

32 **Reincarnated Crane (right).**   Y hooks X's attacking arm with a left Crane Beak, and strikes a vital point behind X's left ear with a right Crane Beak. This is an elegant pattern, and not easy for a student to counter. Without moving leg position, but just by a shift of stance, Y avoids X's attack and simultaneously strikes him or her from behind – *figure 10.5 (d)*.

33 **White Tiger Presents Claw (right).**   X's counter is beautiful too. By turning around into the left False-Leg Stance, he or she avoids Y's attack, and simultaneously grips the vital points at Y's elbow with a right Tiger Claw. This is another example of no defence, direct counter. See *figure 10.5 (e)*.

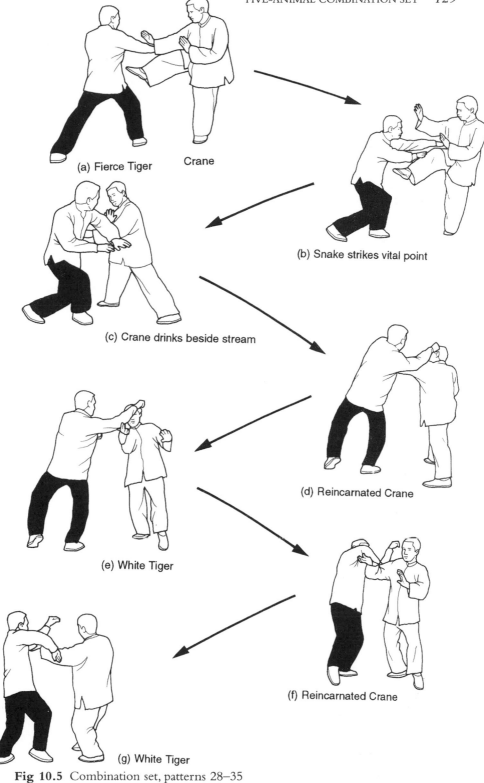

(a) Fierce Tiger   Crane

(b) Snake strikes vital point

(c) Crane drinks beside stream

(d) Reincarnated Crane

(e) White Tiger

(f) Reincarnated Crane

(g) White Tiger

Fig 10.5 Combination set, patterns 28–35

34 **Reincarnated Crane (left).**   By shifting his or her body weight to the left leg and standing in the right False-Leg Stance, Y avoids the Tiger Claw. With a right Crane Beak he or she hooks away X's arm, and simultaneously strikes X's temple with a left Crane Beak – *figure 10.5 (f)*.

35 **White Tiger Presents Claw (left).**   X uses the same tiger pattern against Y's second crane attack, shifting his or her body weight to the left leg and standing in a right False-Leg Stance, simultaneously gripping Y's left elbow. A Tiger Claw gripping the elbow of an attacking crane pattern is a very good counter-attack, employing the principle of using one's strength against the opponent's weakness. This counter is like a tiger gripping a crane's neck. See *figure 10.5 (g)*.

36 **Old Dragon Takes Water.**   Y makes a circular movement with the left hand to push away X's Tiger Claw, and simultaneously strikes X's ribs with a right Dragon Palm – *figure 10.6 (a)*. He or she may need to adjust leg position, for example moving the right leg back, to achieve the best spacing for this purpose.

37 **Golden Leopard Speeds Through Lotus.**   To avoid Y's attack, X moves the left leg across the right leg from behind, makes a left about-turn and sits in a sideways Horseriding Stance, striking out a right Leopard Punch – *figure 10.6 (b)*. This is also a no defence, direct counter.

38 **Double Dragons Play with Pearl.**   Y 'shallows' X's attack by shifting the body to the back right leg, then shoots his front left leg forward into a left Bow-Arrow Stance, simultaneously striking out a Double Dragon attack with the right punch above, and the left punch below, and the palms, if they had been open, facing each other – *figure 10.6 (c)*. This is an example of defence and counter.

39 **Crane Stands Among Cockerels.**   X jumps to the right with the right leg, and kicks at Y's ribs with the left leg, using the toes as striking points – *figure 10.6 (d)*.

40 **Angry Leopard Charges at Rock.**   Y moves the back right leg to the right into a left False-Leg Stance, thus avoiding X's kick, and simultaneously strikes X's ankle with a left Leopard Punch – *figure 10.6 (e)*. Y is about to follow up with another attack, but X has jumped away after pulling the leg back immediately after the kick.

(a) Old Dragon takes water

(b) Golden Leopard

(c) Double Dragons

(d) Crane

(e) Angry Leopard

(f) Lohan   Single Tiger

Fig 10.6 Combination set, patterns 36–42

41 **Poise Patterns.** For their poise patterns, X uses Lohan Asks the Way while Y uses Single Tiger Emerges from Cave – *figure 10.6 (f)*.

42 **Focus Chi at *dan tian*.** Both participants complete the combination set with mutual greetings, followed by focusing chi at their *dan tian* – *figure 10.6 (g)*.

Advanced Techniques to Clinch Victory

The techniques illustrated above are quite advanced. For various reasons, the fighting techniques used today are relatively simple compared to those of the past, and are mostly comprised of elementary punches and kicks, and straightforward blocks. Hence, some people who are used to seeing such simple techniques may question whether the elaborate Shaolin techniques shown above are practical, or whether they are merely flowery movements of use only in prearranged demonstrations. They may doubt whether any person can be skilful enough to apply these complex techniques in a fight.

It is true that if someone gives you a straightforward punch, it is easier to respond with a straightforward block. It needs more skill, which means much more dedicated practice, to respond in the ways demonstrated in the Five-Animal combination set, such as hooking the attacking arm with one Crane Beak and striking the temple with another, or gripping the attacker's wrist in one Tiger Claw and gripping the armpit in another. But it is more combat efficient to employ the more advanced techniques. In a combat situation, if exponents do not use the more efficient advanced techniques, it is because they do not know them, or because they lack the skill to use them effectively.

In the past, when efficient fighting might mean the difference between life and death, combatants would attain very advanced levels of skill and techniques. It was the norm to use advanced techniques, because they are more efficacious than simple ones. Combatants who used simple punches and kicks and elementary blocks (with a few exceptions which will be explained in the next chapter), would easily be defeated, because their simple techniques put them at a disadvantage.

If you are prepared to spend the time and effort to develop these advanced techniques and skills to a high standard, you will easily beat opponents who use only simple punches, kicks and blocks, and whose skills in using them are not as good as yours in executing advanced techniques. When someone punches you, for instance, and you shift your body to one side and grip his or her elbow with your powerful Tiger Claw, that ends the combat. If someone gives you a side kick and you thread away his leg, and follow up with a Leopard Punch at a soft spot below his ribs, this puts the attacker out of action. You can win easily because your opponents, who only know simple punches, kicks and blocks, have never seen such 'outlandish' techniques before. When they meet a master who executes them well, they simply do not know how to react.

But in time, as you use these advanced techniques more often, others will learn and practise ways to overcome them. When you grip someone's elbow with your Tiger Claw, he or she may know how to neutralize it with a circular sweep of one hand and strike you with a Dragon Palm of the other hand. When you drive a Leopard Punch into somebody's soft spot, he or she may grip your wrist, twist it and grip some vital points at your armpit with a Tiger Claw of the other hand. You will have to respond to these counter-attacks, and then they will have to respond to yours. Because you will all have passed beyond the level of simple attack and defence, you will, if you want to win, have to use only techniques; that can give you the best advantage in the different combat situations. In other words, when the level of fighting has become high, most combatants will use techniques like those that were illustrated in the Five-Animal combination set above, because they give the most advantages.

However, techniques are not the only deciding factor in combat. You must have force to back your techniques. For example, you may be able to grip your opponent's elbow or drive a Leopard Punch, but if your grip or punch lacks the force to cause sufficient damage, you will not win. Force training will be explained in the next chapter.

11

THE INTERNAL FORCE OF SHAOLIN KUNG FU

Becoming a Master Through Force Training

❖ *At an advanced level, when the combatants know the right defence for virtually every attack, the decisive factor is often not technique but* gong, *ie force or skill.*

The Relationship Between Technique and Force

Some people have rightly said that awarding black belts in any martial art to children gives a false sense of competence. It is acceptable if they are awarded as an encouragement for their wholesome participation in martial arts as sports or as a recognition of the fact that they have attained certain skills and techniques, but it should not be imagined that children with black belts are formidable fighters to be reckoned with even by adults. In a fight a seven-year-old black belt, for example, will be no match for a powerful adult, even though the child is trained in martial arts techniques and the adult may have no knowledge of martial arts at all. Even though the child may hit the adult many times, it will not cause any serious injury, but just one powerful blow by the adult may be sufficient to kill the child. The decisive factor here is force.

In terms of force, the relationship between a Kung Fu master and an ordinary person is like that between a powerful adult and a child. With the exception of vital spots like the eye, throat and genitals, which will be carefully guarded, a master with the art of Iron Fist and Iron Shirt, for example, can take hits from an ordinary person without sustaining injury, but a single strike of the Iron Fist, which can create a hole in a wall, will also break bones and damage internal organs.

Hence, the mark of a master lies in depth of force rather than range of techniques. Of course, this does not mean that techniques are not important; it only shows that force is generally a more significant factor in deciding victory in combat. When the question of force is not relevant, as when children fight among themselves, or when students of similar force levels engage in sparring, techniques become very important.

The word 'force' is an imperfect translation of the Chinese term *gong* (pronounced 'kung'). The term 'Kung Fu' (*gongfu* in Romanized Chinese) comes from this concept of *gong*, indicating that the emphasis is not on learning techniques but on training force. Besides force, the concept of *gong* also includes other factors like skill, speed, agility, balance, fluidity of movement and correctness of form.

For convenience, *gong* may be classified into different types, such as basic and specialized, hard and soft, external and internal, but this classification is arbitrary and provisional, and there is often much overlap.

Briefly, basic *gong* or basic skills refer to the fundamental Kung Fu skills like stances, balance and agility which constitute the foundation of all development. Specialized *gong* or specialized arts refer to skills and force that are usually limited to specific functions, like the art of Tiger Claw for effective, powerful grip, and the art of Running on Grass, which is a figurative way of saying the exponent can run very fast.

Hard *gong* or hard force refers to force that usually exhibits great destructive power, like Iron Fist and Iron Palm. It is mainly acquired through hard (meaning both tough and difficult) conditioning, like hitting sandbags and jabbing the palm into granules for years. Soft *gong* or soft arts, in contrast, are developed through more gentle, but not necessarily easy, means, like repeatedly stretching and bending the muscles as in the art of Flexible Legs, to develop quick, subtle muscular movements, and running in a maze of poles as in the art of Running Through Woods, to develop agility.

External *gong* or external force is developed through external means, like hitting sandbags, striking poles, carrying weights, stretching muscles and running on the rims of huge baskets. Internal *gong* or internal force is derived from internal methods, principally by means of strengthening *jing* (matter in its finest form), controlling chi (vital energy), and developing *shen* (mind).

Generally, but not always, hard force is developed by external methods, and internal arts are soft. Hence it is common to equate hard with external and soft with internal. But we must remember that some hard force, like Golden Bell where the exponent can take even weapon attacks without sustaining injury, is internal; and many forms of soft, internal force like Cosmos Palm and One-Finger Zen can be very powerful. The word 'soft' is a poor translation of the Chinese term *rou*, which does not imply any lack of force. The training of advanced Shaolin arts generally involves both external and internal, hard and soft methods.

Basic skills are very important. Many students overlook them, thinking that they are elementary, but in fact, both the terms 'basic' and 'elementary' suggest that they lay the foundation for future development. If you want to become a Kung Fu master, you should spend some time on basic skills, especially the Horseriding Stance and the art of Flexible Legs, as explained in Chapter 6. Two other very important basic exercises, the arts of One-Finger Shooting Zen and Thirty Punches, are explained below.

The Art of One-Finger Shooting Zen

The One-Finger Zen hand form is a representative Shaolin symbol, and the art of One-Finger Shooting Zen is the fundamental force training technique in my Shaolin school, the Shaolin Wahnam Kung Fu and Chi Kung School, founded by me and named after my two masters, Sifu Lai Chin Wah and Sifu Ho Fatt Nam, who so kindly and generously passed the Shaolin arts to me.

The words of my master Sifu Ho Fatt Nam, when I first learned Shaolin Kung Fu from him, still ring in my ears. He said:

> One-Finger Zen and Tiger Claw are two of the most advanced arts in Shaolin Kung Fu. They are found in the art of One-Finger Shooting Zen. Continue to practise this art daily even after you have become a master.

Ideally you should practise the art of Shooting Zen after you can sit in the Horseriding Stance for five minutes. To save time, you may begin it when you can perform the Horseriding Stance well, but you *must* continue practising the stance until you can achieve the minimum five minutes.

1 Sit comfortably in a Horseriding Stance. Gently sink your chi to your abdominal *dan tian*, the energy field about 3in below your navel. Hold your right One-Finger Zen hand form near your breast, with the index finger pointing skyward – *figure 11.1 (a)*. Breathe in gently through your nose.

2 Gently move the One-Finger Zen forward until your arm is fully extended, but without your elbow locked, and your arm is parallel to the ground at shoulder level – *figure 11.1 (b)*. Do not raise your shoulder. As you move your arm out, gently breathe out through your mouth with a gentle 'shsss...' sound coming from your kidneys.

3 Then bring your One-Finger Zen back to the starting position – *figure 11.1 (a)*, gently breathing in as you do so.

4 Repeat this moving out and bringing in of your One-Finger Zen twice, ie three times altogether.

5 After doing this three times, shoot out your One-Finger Zen with some speed and let your index finger point forwards, with your arm straight – *figure 11.1 (c)*. Simultaneously let out an explosive 'her-it' sound, coming from your abdomen. Make sure that you do not raise your shoulder.

6 Change your hand form from the One-Finger Zen to a Tiger Claw. Bend your arm slightly and make a clockwise circle with your Tiger Claw in front of your body, as if you were blocking an opponent's punch – *figure 11.2 (a)*.

7 Then pull your right Tiger Claw down near to your right knee – *figure 11.2 (b)* – simultaneously making a 'yaa...' sound, vibrating from your lungs.

8 Relax fully with a 'ha' sound. Hold your right hand in a fist and place it at your waist. Swallow the saliva in your mouth into your stomach, and feel it go down to your abdomen.

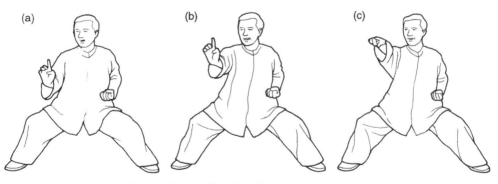

Fig 11.1 The art of One-Finger Shooting Zen

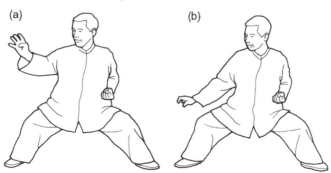

Fig 11.2 Tiger Claw in One-Finger Shooting Zen

9 Now use your left hand to repeat the whole process. Then repeat the whole procedure, right and left hand, many times – the number of times depends on your progress.

10 When you can co-ordinate your breathing and movement well in your Horseriding Stance, progress to the next stage. Perform the same procedure, except that when you move your hand out and breathe out, visualize your vital energy flowing from your abdominal *dan tian* to your index finger. When you move your hand in and breathe in, visualize cosmic energy flowing into your *dan tian*.

11 Next, when you can co-ordinate your mind, energy flow and hand movement well, progress to the final stage of channelling internal force. Perform the same procedure, but as you move your hand out and in, tense it and visualize it as charged with internal force. As you shoot out your One-Finger Zen, visualize your internal force shooting out like an arrow. You need not worry about what internal force is; when it comes you will experience it, and it can be so powerful that your index finger will vibrate naturally with the force.

12 At the end of the One-Finger Shooting Zen, drop your arms to your side with the palms open, and bend your body slightly – *figure 11.3 (a)*.

13 Jump lightly to bring both feet centrally together. As you jump, bring both hands to breast level, with the palms facing upwards – *figure 11.3 (b)* – and simultaneously breathe in through your nose, into your chest.

14 Then turn your palms face down, and lower them – *figure 11.3 (c)*, so that your arms drop naturally at your sides. At the same time, breathe out gently through your mouth, and let your chi sink gently, very gently, down to your abdominal *dan tian* – *figure 11.3 (d)*.

15 Close your eyes and relax. Do not think of anything. Remain in this standing meditation position for a few minutes. If you have been practising the Shooting Zen correctly, you will feel internal force flowing along your arms as well as swelling inside you.

16 Finally rub your palms together, warm your eyes with your palms as you open them, massage your face and head gently, and walk about briskly. This is the standard procedure to complete most forms of force training.

It is very important that even though you tense your arm and finger, you must never *be* tense, especially in your chest. The relaxation with a 'ha' sound at the completion of each set of movements is very important. If you feel pain in your chest, it means you have been performing the exercise incorrectly, and you must stop, at least for the time being. Serious injury may result if you persist despite the warning sign of pain. A self-manifested chi flow exercise, which will be explained in Chapter 14, can relieve this problem.

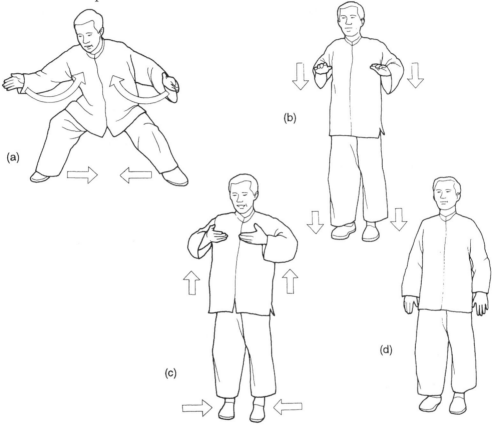

Fig 11.3 Feeling the swell of internal force

Developing Forceful Punches

The art of Thirty Punches consists of three stages: empty punching, punching with weights and punching a sandbag. You should proceed to the next stage only after you have attained some force in the previous ones. There is no time limit for the duration of training in this art, but a minimum is two months for each stage.

1 Sit comfortably in a Horseriding Stance. Breathe in gently through your nose, into your abdominal *dan tian*.

2 Punch out your right fist, letting out an explosive 'her-it' sound at the same time – *figure 11.4 (a)*. Make sure you do not move your body, especially your shoulder.

3 Hold the punch for two or three seconds, and breathe in gently into your *dan tian*.

4 Repeat the procedure alternating your left and right fist for thirty punches. Complete the training with the standard procedure as explained in the section on One-Finger Shooting Zen above.

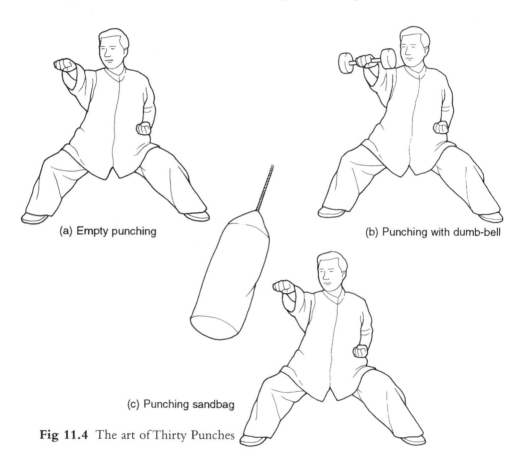

(a) Empty punching

(b) Punching with dumb-bell

(c) Punching sandbag

Fig 11.4 The art of Thirty Punches

When you can punch quite well without moving your shoulder, punch with all your might. Imagine that you are knocking down a wall each time you punch. Later, instead of taking a breath for each punch, one breath can last for three consecutive punches, without losing any force. Then you can progress to one breath for five punches, seven punches and so on. In this way you will also increase the speed of your punch, without reducing your punching force. This completes the stage of empty punching.

The second stage is similar to the first, except that you hold weights in your fist while punching. In the past, students used stone-locks, which were self-made cement blocks with bars across as handles. Modern students can use the more convenient dumb-bells – *figure 11.4 (b)*. Start with a comfortable weight, then work up gradually to heavier ones.

In the third stage, sit in a Horseriding Stance and punch a hanging sandbag 30 times. That is one set, and you can train for many sets. Your punch should be so powerful that you send the sandbag flying with each punch – *figure 11.4 (c)*. Gradually increase the weight of the sandbag.

If you are ambitious and train for three years instead of six months, you can use marbles and pebbles, then ball bearings and iron filings, instead of sand for your punching bags. You will then have progressed from the art of Thirty Punches to Iron Fist.

In developing hard, external force like Iron Fist, or even punching a sandbag in Thirty Punches, it is necessary to apply Kung Fu medicine to prevent or cure any injury. The following medicinal wine is useful for relieving injuries like bruises, pain, swelling, blood clots, energy blockages at the superficial level, and other traumatic injuries sustained through hard force training or sparring. The names of the ingredients in Chinese are as follows:

ru xiang, mo yao, chuan hong hua, gui wei, zhi ke, chuan gong, tao ren, mu xiang, chen xiang, jin jie, chi yao, ji geng, zhi zi, hu gu, dan pi.

Take 12g of each ingredients and soak the mixture in 3 pints of white rice wine. After about two months, discard the residue. Rub some medicinal wine externally on the injured spot, and avoid bringing the medicated part into contact with water for at least an hour.

While Iron Fist was a formidable asset in the past, in my opinion its great destructive properties limit its practical usefulness in today's more settled times. Indeed, when one is likely to break bones or even kill someone with one punch, Iron Fist becomes a liability instead of an asset. The long training time needed to develop it would be better spent on other Shaolin arts, some of which will be described later, which will bring benefits to you and others. If you want an art that is forceful in self-defence, but will not destroy your opponent, *qin-na* and Tiger Claw would be a good choice.

The Compassionate Art of *Qin-Na*

The Shaolin arts of *qin-na* and Tiger Claw, in line with the spirit of Shaolin teaching, represent a compassionate way of fighting, because they can be used to defeat or subdue opponents decisively without hurting them unnecessarily. There are three ways of attacking using the Tiger Claw: jabbing the claws right into the body, striking with the Tiger Claw palm, and gripping the opponent with the Tiger Claw.

The first method is savage, usually resulting in the opponent's death, and it is therefore never used by Shaolin masters. The second method uses the internal force of the tiger and often causes serious injury, although the opponent can usually recover by taking Kung Fu medicine. It is seldom used. The most popular way of using the Tiger Claw is the third way, holding and gripping, known in Chinese as *qin-na*. It puts an opponent out of action, yet he or she can recover almost immediately.

Qin-na is technically and qualitatively different from the holds and locks found in some other martial arts, although they may appear to be similar superficially. It actually consists of two parts: *qin*, which means 'hold', and *na* which may be translated as 'grip'. Although closely related, they are two different techniques. *Na*, as far as I know, is unique in Shaolin Kung Fu. It is not found in any other martial arts, at least not in as refined and deep a way as Shaolin Kung Fu. *Na*, as used here, is not just 'grip' as in gripping somebody's hand or gripping an umbrella in an ordinary manner, in which case it would be no different from *qin* or 'hold'. *Na* involves gripping in a special way with the fingers penetrating deep into the opponent's vital points, tendons or joints, so that any unpractised attempt by the opponent to pull away would result in more injury. A *qin-na* exponent needs to know the meridian system, vital points and positions of the muscles, tendons and joints of the body in detail. There is no English equivalent for *qin-na*; the convenient translation 'hold and grip' gives only a partial idea.

Many people, including martial artists, are unaware that when you hold an opponent even in an elaborate lock, you yourself are being immobilized as much as your opponent. As soon as you release your hold to free yourself, your opponent becomes free to fight you again. This is not the case in *qin-na*, because your penetrating grip, not your hold, immobilizes the opponent, so that even when you release the hold he will be unable to fight effectively. Hence, in *qin-na* it is not necessary to employ elaborate locks; an apparently simple grip on the elbow, for example, as is shown in the combination set in the previous chapter, is sufficient to put the opponent out of action, because it will have damaged the vital points or tendons controlling the mobility of the arm.

Qin-na works on three main principles, concisely expressed as 'separating tendons', 'dislocating joints' and 'gripping points'. They refer to techniques of immobilizing the opponent by damaging his tendons and muscles that control body movement, displacing the natural functions of the joints, and blocking energy flow (including the flow of mental impulses along nerves) at vital points that affect the reactions. If you damage the muscles of the upper arm, for example, or dislocate the elbow, or grip some vital points at the shoulder, you can put that arm out of action.

But this injury is only temporary; a master can restore the opponent's natural functions almost immediately, for example by massaging the affected muscles, fixing the dislocation and releasing the energy blockages at the vital points. Dislocating joints is not often used because there is a risk involved. The following advice from my master, Sifu Ho Fatt Nam, when he taught me *qin-na*, is invaluable:

> If we are not accurate, or if the opponent moves at just the wrong time when we dislocate the arm, portions from the head of the bone may be broken off. It is easy to replace a dislocation or to fix a fracture of the body of the bone but to fix a fractured bone-head is extremely difficult. If it is not properly done, the opponent may suffer for life. We do not want that to happen.

To apply *qin-na* well, besides knowing the techniques and having the skill to reach the right spots accurately, it is necessary to have the internal force to execute the techniques. The type of force used to back up *qin-na* is usually Tiger Claw or Eagle Claw, both of which are famous Shaolin arts. We do not have enough space to go further into this effective, compassionate art, and to discuss *qin-na* techniques, their effects on various parts of the body and remedial measures to relieve injuries, but training for its back-up force, Tiger Claw, is explained below. And even if you do not know the intricacies of *qin-na*, the Tiger Claw force is very useful.

The Internal Force of Tiger Claw

1 Stand in a right Bow-Arrow Stance. Without moving your body, swing both palms, with fingers slightly bent, from your left side up to your front as if you were performing the Mirror Hand block, with your

right palm at about eye level, and your left palm near your right elbow – *figure 11.5 (a)*. Simultaneously let out a 'her-it' sound, coming from your abdomen.

2 Turn both palms so that they now face away from you and holding them in the Tiger Claw hand form pull them downwards, with your right Tiger Claw at about your right knee, and your left at about your left knee – *figure 11.5 (b)*. Simultaneously let out a continuous 'yaa...' sound, as you tense your hand and channel internal force to your fingers.

3 Relax after you have pulled your Tiger Claws down to your knees.

4 Repeat three times. For beginners, practising three times may be quite strenuous if the exercise is done correctly.

5 Rest for a short while, and perform the exercises another three times on your left side using a left Bow-Arrow Stance.

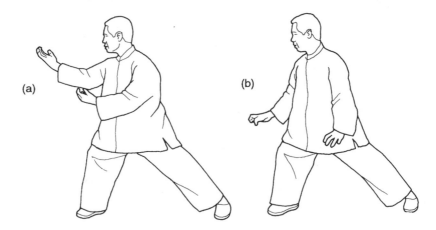

(a)   (b)

Fig 11.5 Fierce Tiger Cleanses Claws

This exercise is called Fierce Tiger Cleanses Claws, and should be be practised throughout your Tiger Claw training. As you progress, gradually increase the number of times you do it, and skip the short rest between the right and left mode of training. Later, instead of turning from the right to the left Bow-Arrow Stance, move your back left leg forward to form a left Bow-Arrow Stance, then move your back right leg forward to form a right Bow-Arrow Stance, while you continue to perform the exercise. Then reverse the movement; move your front right leg backwards to form a left Bow-Arrow Stance. You may move forwards or backwards after one or more 'cleansing' exercises. Remember to adjust the position of your feet as you change stances.

Later you can use other stances and move in different directions. But it is very important to relax after each 'claw cleansing', and you must not feel pain in your chest after your training. Practise for at least three months before proceeding to the next stage, but still continue with this exercise throughout the whole Tiger Claw training period.

The next exercise involves jabbing your hands into a container of beans. Fill a basin or box about three-quarters full with black beans and green beans in about equal proportion. Place it on a table or chair at a suitable height. Stand in the Horseriding Stance in front of it, hold up your palms, and channel internal force to your fingers. Take a deep breath into your abdominal *dan tian* and jab your palms, with the fingers apart, straight into the beans as in *figure 11.6*, breathing out at the same time. It is advisable to cover your face with a piece of cloth to prevent dust from the beans getting into your mouth and nose.

At first you may reach only a few inches into the beans, but gradually aim to reach the bottom. After each jabbing, grip the beans with your palms, turn them face up, raise them high above the beans, then turn again and strike downward onto the beans with your palms. Repeat about 20–30 times, and gradually increase the repetition as you progress.

Fig 11.6 Jabbing the hands into beans

You should practise this exercise for at least six months. Remember to practise Fierce Tiger Cleanses Claws over the same period. If you sustain any external injury in the training, such as bruised or sprained fingers, apply the medicinal wine mentioned earlier.

Meridians (pathways of energy flow inside our body) in our hands are connected to our eyes and other organs. Faulty practice in this jabbing exercise can cause energy blockage that may affect our eyes. This is an example of how training without proper guidance (from a master or a good book) may result in harmful side-effects. The risk of energy blockages and harmful side-effects can be effectively overcome with the exercises described below. Chi Kung exercises like Lifting the Sky and the Self-Manifested Chi Movement (see Chapter 14) are also excellent.

After jabbing, gripping and striking the beans, complete the exercise using the standard procedure as explained in the section on One-Finger Shooting Zen. Then move away so that bean dust would not get into your nose, remove your face cloth, stand upright and relax. With your arms dropping straight (but not strained) at your sides, flex or stretch your fingers as far and wide as possible 49 times. Then close your eyes and enjoy standing meditation for a few minutes. This finger-stretching exercise is derived from the Classic of Sinew Metamorphosis taught by the great Bodhidharma, the first Patriarch of the Shaolin arts.

Either immediately after this exercise or at another time, you can move on to the next stage. Stand at a suitable distance from a tree or plant with green leaves. Use your eyes to count the leaves. Start with 50, then gradually over a few weeks work up to 200. After counting leaves roll your eyeballs slowly in a wide circle three times clockwise and three times anticlockwise without moving your head.

After this exercise, called Rolling Stars, close your eyes and 'nourish your *shen*'. This involves standing upright for a few minutes, resting your eyes, relaxing without thinking of anything, and spontaneously (ie without any conscious effort) letting your mind expand. This set of exercises – Counting Leaves, Rolling Stars and Nourishing *Shen* – is wonderful; you can practise them by themselves as well as part of the Tiger Claw training. Many people have commended me on my good eyesight despite my age and these exercises have a lot to do with it.

The next stage is Taming the Tiger, which is push-ups using Tiger Claws for support. With your body straight and supported only by the fingers of your hands and the toes of your feet as in – *figure 11.7 (a)*, bend your elbows so that your chest is almost touching the ground – *figure 11.7 (b)*. Then straighten your arms so that you return to the original position. Repeat this about 5–10 times, then gradually increase to 50 times.

You can either breathe out while you lower your body and in while you raise it, or vice versa, but you must keep to the same pattern throughout the training session. You can then change it for a different session if you wish. Practise this exercise for at least three months.

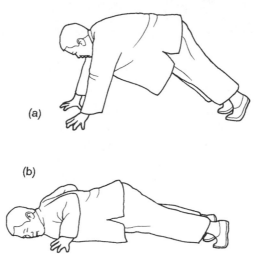

(a)

(b)

Fig 11.7 Taming the Tiger

The next stage is called Gripping Jars. Get two large jars with small round openings so that you can hold each with one hand by gripping its opening with your fingers. Grip the two jars and hold them with your arms straight at shoulder level, and walk about or move in different stances for a few minutes – *figure 11.8*. You can also move the jars about, still gripped by the fingers. Add a cup of water to the jars every three days. When they are full of water, continue the training by adding a cup of sand every three days. You should practise this exercise for at least six months.

Fig 11.8 Gripping Jars with Tiger Claws

The time I have suggested you spend on Tiger Claw training, as with that for other courses, is the minimum required to attain a reasonably high standard. Of course the more time you spend on it, the better or more powerful your art or force will become. In the Tiger Claw training, you can continue practising any of the stages even after you have completed the minimum requirement.

If some of the training aids are not available, you can skip one or two stages, but that will mean that your training will be incomplete and your force less powerful. But it will still be adequate for the modern, less demanding standards. You must practise the finger-stretching exercise and eye exercises if you perform the bean-jabbing exercise, however, and you must practise Fierce Tiger Cleanses Claws, which develops internal force, throughout the training period.

At the student level, someone who has a good knowledge of techniques and is able to apply them in combat will usually win, both in sparring and in real fights. At an advanced level, when the combatants know the right defence for virtually every attack, the decisive factor is often not technique but *gong*, ie force or skill. An advanced practitioner loses a fight not because of ignorance of the right counters, but because, despite a knowledge of the appropriate defence techniques they cannot be effectively implemented because of the greater force or skill of the opponent.

12

TACTICS AND STRATEGIES

Creating Opportunities to Defeat Your Opponent

❖ *What would you do to ensure victory if you met a competent opponent who did not give you any technical advantage? You would have to create the advantages yourself.*

Techniques, Tactics and Strategies

If you want to be effective in combat, you must ensure that you do not give away unnecessary advantages to your opponent. If your vital spots are unguarded when you attack, or if your balance is poor when you defend, you have put yourself at a disadvantage without any effort on your opponent's part. Such mistakes are common among students.

At a higher level, when you have become proficient in guarding your own weakness, you should look for and exploit your opponent's mistakes. In other words, when you need not worry about whether you have left any spot exposed or whether your defence movements are clumsy because correctness of form and fluidity of movement have become second nature to you even in combat, you should seek out these very weakness in your opponent and exploit them. This, indeed, is one of the main differences between a master and a novice, and a master will often defeat an opponent on this count. For example, when an opponent is awkward in a particular situation, the master can exploit this weakness at the right time and defeat the opponent with a simple technique which in an ordinary situation could be defended against.

But what would you do to ensure victory if you met a competent opponent who did not give you any technical advantage? You would have to create the advantages yourself. You can do so by using appropriate tactics and strategies. Even when your opponent is superior to you, a skilful use of tactics and strategies can reverse the balance of advantage.

Knowing and practising the following three steps in combat will help you to become a good fighter:

1 Ensure that your form and movement are flawless so that you do not give away unnecessary technical advantages to your opponent.
2 Seek weakness in your opponent's form and movement and exploit them to your advantages.
3 Create advantages for yourself by the skilful use of tactics and strategies.

For our purposes, tactics refer to a planned application of techniques in certain general ways to secure advantages, or in some situations to minimize disadvantages. A strategy is a design to manipulate an opponent into responding in certain ways so as to implement the tactics or achieve the objectives you want.

For example, if you meet an opponent like an expert boxer, who is very fast with his punches, you would be at a disadvantage if you fought him in ways he is used to, like blocking his punches and attacking with your own. On the other hand, you could gain the advantage if you focused on attacking his legs and abdomen, for those would be his weak spots. So a good tactic would be to avoid his punches, for example by squatting down, and attack his lower body by sweeping his leg or kicking up at his abdomen while you are on the ground.

But how would you put this tactic into practice? If you start by dropping to the ground straight away and sweeping or kicking him, a good tactic would be wasted by poor implementation. Your opponent would just jump away, as a boxer can very easily do. In other words, although your tactic would be good, you would not have strategy. A good strategy might be to pretend to use your hands the way he does, but without blocking his punches or attacking him, and do not use patterns like Beauty Looks at Mirror and Black Tiger Steals Heart.

You could pretend to block and punch, while spacing yourself in such a way that even without blocking, his punches could not reach you. Your own punches would also not really be meant to hit him; the main purpose would be to tempt him to continue attacking you, while you mostly retreat. Suddenly, when he least expected it and while he was concentrating on his attack, you would move down and strike him from below.

This strike would have to be decisive, putting him out of action with just one blow. With an expert boxer you could not afford to take chances. Of course you should not hurt him unnecessarily, a forceful sweep at his knee or a hard kick at his abdominal *dan tian* would be enough to stop him from further aggression. Ignorant onlookers might say how lucky you were, but those who knew would realize that you had employed tactics and strategy expertly.

The Legacy of Past Masters

Do masters formulate their tactics and strategies while actually engaged in combat? They normally do not; doing so would distract them from concentrating on the contest. Through their long years of fighting experience, Shaolin masters throughout the centuries have worked out many effective principles which can serve as tactics and strategies. Thus, the tactics and strategies used by a Shaolin disciple during combat are not impromptu inventions of the moment, but an intelligent application of principles generalized by some of the best warriors in the past from their real fighting experience, and passed on to us as a part of the rich Shaolin tradition. All of these principles, it is interesting to note, are applicable not only in individual fighting but also in mass warfare; after all, many Shaolin masters were famous army generals.

Some of these principles are listed below, starting with simple ones which even beginners can apply. The distinction between tactics and strategies are for the convenience of study; the same principle may be classified as a tactic, a strategy or both, depending on how we intend to use it.

1 Attack continously.
2 Signal to the east, strike to the west.
3 Avoid an opponent's strong points, strike the weak ones.
4 Trick an opponent into advancing without success; strike decisively with just one blow.
5 If an opponent is strong, enter from the side; if he or she is weak, enter from the front.
6 Use four *tahils* against a thousand *katis*, ie use minimum force to neutralize maximum strength.

Suppose you attack your opponent using a right Poisonous Snake Shoots Venom. He or she responds with Beauty Looks at Mirror. Then you attack again using the same snake pattern, but with your left hand. Again he or she responds successfully with a Mirror Hand. It is easy for your opponent to defend against your right and left snake attacks.

Now use the same two attacking patterns, but apply the simple tactic of continuous attack. Strike out your right snake hand. As soon as your opponent's Mirror Hand pushes away your first attack, strike out your left snake hand. If you try this with 10 partners who are at your level, the chances are that you will hit them at least seven times out of 10. 'Hit' here, of course, means that you stop your striking hand a few inches from the target.

The two attacks should flow continuously, as if they were one. But you must not start your second attack too early; start only when the Mirror Hand pushes away your first attack. You should practise with your imaginary opponent before attempting the tactic with your partners.

You need not repeat the same attack patterns for this tactic. You may, for example, strike your opponent with Black Tiger Steals Heart, and as soon as he or she lifts an arm to block your strike, execute a whirlwind kick to the ribs (taking care, once again, to stop a few inches from target). You can work out other combinations yourself.

Using Continuous Attack Effectively

You should be aware of the following points if you want to use the continuous attack tactic efficiently. First, you must be familiar with the form and movement of the patterns you want to use in your continuous attack combination. If your whirlwind kick is not skilful, for instance, using it in your tactic will mean giving an unnecessary advantage to your opponent.

Secondly, your first attack can be real or feigned. If you use a Black Tiger punch and your opponent does not or cannot defend against it, then this first attack becomes real, giving you a successful strike. If the opponent successfully defends against it, it becomes a feigned move, paving the way for your second attack.

Whether you should continue with your second attack if you have hit your opponent with your first will depend on the situation. If your hit causes the opponent to lose balance, you could continue your whirlwind kick, knocking him or her to the ground. However, if the ribs are not exposed because your opponent has not lifted a hand to block your Black Tiger punch, and if he or she is still stable despite your strike, it may not be advantageous to carry on with your whirlwind kick; if you do, you may hit the upper arm but your opponent may be able to put out a hand to attack your exposed genitals. It is therefore necessary to practise these possibilities, called variations in combat sequence training, with your imaginary opponent before you try out the tactic with a partner.

Thirdly, while blocking is the most common response to your punch, you must be ready for other methods of defence. You can often still implement the continuous attack even if your opponent uses a different defence pattern, but you may have to make appropriate variations, which you should have prepared beforehand. For example, your opponent may retreat instead of blocking. You should then move forward to narrow the gap in preparation for your kick later, and execute an extra punch. If your opponent blocks, you kick; if he or she does not block, you may still kick, after you have pushed up his arm. This further illustrates the need for some prior training with your imaginary opponent.

The fourth point is very important. In your attack, you must remember to include provision for your own defence. Shaolin teaching insists that one must not be so wrapped up with attack that one neglects one's defence. Your opponent may, for example, neither block nor dodge, but just shift the body slightly to one side and counter-attack your underside with a Leopard or a Phoenix-Eye Punch, employing the no defence, direct counter. If you have prepared yourself well, you can now turn the tables by dropping the elbow of your attacking hand to guard your underside and inflicting your planned whirlwind kick.

It is necessary to practise all these variations to support the apparently simple tactic of continuous attack. All four of these points apply to the other tactics and strategies listed above. Moreover, while some of the easier principles may be attempted by students at a basic level, their successful implementation requires a high standard in the areas of specific techniques, combat sequences, combination sets, and force training.

A Tactic to Distract Your Opponent

Although continuous attack appears to be similar to signalling to the east, striking to the west, they actually work on different principles. The first depends on continuity of attack, whereas the second depends on distraction.

You might, for example, attack your opponent's upper body with Poisonous Snake Shoots Venom. As he or she responds to this 'upper' attack, lower your stance and strike the lower body with Precious Duck Swims Through Lotus. Or you might attack with a left whirlwind kick, and when your opponent attempts to defend, change to a *right* whirlwind kick.

It is not essential to employ this tactic in pairs of patterns. You may, for example, execute a series of punches, and when your opponent is concentrating on defending against these hand attacks, suddenly deliver an unexpected kick.

Moreover, distraction need not be confined only to attacks. When you meet someone who commonly uses side kicks, for instance, you may combine this tactic with the strategy of tricking the opponent into advancing without success, and striking decisively with one blow. You might pretend to be unskilled in your defence against kicks, and retreat clumsily whenever you are attacked. Having created a false impression of inadequacy, stop retreating and strike the extended, kicking leg with Lohan Strikes Drum, fracturing his leg or dislocating his knee joint. All the four crucial points mentioned earlier, apply to this and other tactics and strategies.

Avoiding an opponent's strong points, and striking the weak ones is both a tactical and strategic principle which is used generally in all combat. In the example of the fast, powerful boxer mentioned at the start of this chapter, this principle is used as a tactic, and the principle of tricking the opponent into attacking without success and then striking him decisively is employed as a strategy.

As I have said, however, the distinction between tactics and strategies is purely for convenience; there is a lot of overlap, and we should not be unduly concerned about the labels. What is more important is the application of these principles to help us to be proficient in combat. We make the distinction to remind ourselves that besides the practical selection of appropriate techniques to achieve our combat objectives, which we call tactics, we also need to consider all the relevant factors philosophically so that these techniques can be effectively applied, which we call strategy. In Chinese, principles are called *xin te*, which means literally 'obtained from the heart', suggesting that they are derived after deep thought; tactics are *fang fa*, literally 'general methods'; and strategies are *zhan lue*, meaning 'discussion for fighting'.

Selecting Strategies to Suit Particular Situations

Suppose you are small and you meet a large, powerful opponent who specializes in throws. If you fight normally you will be at a disadvantage. So you decide to use as a general combat plan the principle of avoiding the opponent's strong points and attacking the weak ones. But how do you implement this strategy? If your attacker moves in to catch you so as to throw you, for example, what techniques should you use to avoid the attack? And how would you counter-attack?

A quick review of the principles listed above would suggest that using four *tahils* against a thousand *katis*, or using minimum force to neutralize maximum strength would be a good tactic. You know that engaging the opponent from the front is no good; so you also employ the tactic of moving in from the side. You then select techniques that will help you put these tactics into effect.

Thus, even before either of you has made a move, you have a good idea of how you are going to fight – your strategy – and what patterns you are going to use to get the best technical advantages – your tactics. Despite your apparent disadvantage in terms of strength and size, you are now in a better position than an opponent who has not made any pre-combat assessment, and therefore has no guidelines to fight to. He or she is like a general sending in an army without any plans.

Guided by your strategy and tactics, you will not engage in close-body fighting, for that will give the opponent the oportunity to catch and throw you. When he or she moves in to attack, you will not block, for that may allow him or her to catch hold of your hands, but instead will jump aside and counter-attack with fast jabs or kicks. As soon as you have made an attack you will move away quickly, giving the opponent little chance to close in on you.

If your arm is caught, you will aim your other hand at weak spots like the eyes or throat as a distraction, and simultaneously turn your arm in a circle against the finger joints to release the hold – a technique implementing the tactic of using four *tahils* to neutralize a thousand *katis* – giving your opponent no time to throw you. Your response will be a reflex action because, knowing that the opponent's strong point is attack by throwing, you will have prepared for such an eventuality beforehand.

You will also have prepared for the possibility of your opponent catching your leg when you kick. If that happens you will step on the opponent's thigh for support, climb onto his or her back like a monkey and strike the eyes and throat. (As always, of course, you would not actually cause any damage, but stop just in front of the target.)

Now let us reverse the situation. Suppose you are big and strong, and your opponent is small. Now that you have the upper hand, does it follow that if you use the same strategy and tactics, it will be even easier for you to win? Not at all. If you use the same strategy and tactics, you will be at a disadvantage because they are meant for use by smaller people against large ones.

When you are fighting from a position of strength, a suitable strategy might be to bulldoze straight into your opponent and attack the strongest point, which will still be weaker than yours.

If your opponent's strong point is hand attacks or kicks, for example, you need not worry about such intricacies as shifting your body sideways to avoid a direct impact or making a circular movement to minimize the force. If you want to block, block head on; or better still, strike the attacking arm or leg directly. If the opponent tries to hold you or to fell you, which are not wise moves for a smaller person against a bigger one, merely flick away the hold or sit firmly in your stance, then strike with a straight, powerful punch.

This does not mean that you can afford to be careless with a smaller or weaker opponent, however. Even if you bulldoze into the attack, you must not forget to consider your response to any counter-attacks.

Understanding strategies and tactics, therefore, makes a big difference in combat. But strategies and tactics are guidelines; basically you must still have the skill and force to implement them.

13

CLASSICAL KUNG FU WEAPONS

How to Tell a Sword from a Knife

❖ *No other martial arts in the world can boast of a range of weapons as wide or as varied as that in Shaolin Kung Fu.*

Why are Classical Weapons Still Being Practised?

An interesting feature of Shaolin Kung Fu is its weaponry. No other martial arts in the world can boast of a range of weapons as wide or as varied as that in Shaolin Kung Fu. In most martial arts today students learn mainly unarmed combat, with some techniques for use against armed opponents. In Shaolin Kung Fu there are complete weapon sets which are as important as unarmed sets in the standard curriculum. In the past weapon sets were even more important than unarmed ones. This was natural at the time, as who would not use a weapon to fight if it could be carried freely?

However, carrying a weapon is now illegal in most countries. Why then, you may ask, learn to fight with weapons if you are not likely to use them in real combat?

There are many good reasons why classical weapons are still being taught today, although many people who practise them may not know them! If you ask a Kung Fu instructor why he or she teaches classical weapons, he or she may say that it is part of the Kung Fu tradition, and Kung Fu training without weapons is incomplete. Teaching classical weapons can also be a good way to attract students, since many people find learning about these beautiful, sometimes strange, weapons interesting, and practising them gives a class a distinct Kung Fu flavour, as there are no such elaborate, impressive weapons in other martial arts systems.

There are, of course, other reasons more relevant to self-defence. Nowadays you do not lash a sword behind your back or grasp a spear in your hands and walk about the streets, as many Kung Fu exponents did in the past. But in a fight, even under ordinary circumstances and in ordinary places, you can often find a piece of wood or a sharpened pole that can be used, even if only clumsily, as a rod or a spear. Moreover, if other people use such improvised weapons against you, you will be able to deal with them more competently if you have learned the principles and properties of their classical counterparts in weapon sets. Many modern improvised weapons are images of classical ones. A broken bottle acts like a dagger, a bicycle chain like a soft whip, a heavy object like a round hammer, an ordinary chair like a Kung Fu bench.

If you carry weights while you practise your unarmed sets, you will not only find it more tiring, but you will also find that you can further increase your stamina and power. Practising weapon sets is similar to this in many ways, and you will probably prefer to hold novel and often fanciful weapons, rather than dull dumb-bells. Some special skills are required for, or achieved through, the use of certain weapons, and these skills are generally also helpful in unarmed combat. In practising with long, heavy weapons like the trident or the Guan knife, for example, you need stable stances, or else you may swing yourself off the ground. These stable stances, consolidated by training in weapon sets, are transferable to and useful in unarmed combat, enabling you to swing an opponent off the ground.

Staffs

There are two main types of staffs: long staffs, which are about 7ft long and short staffs, which measure about 5ft. Long staffs are almost always tapered, and are sometimes called mouse-tail staffs because of their shape. Short staffs are seldom tapered, and are thus sometimes called double-headed staffs.

The long staffs originated from the long spears carried by classical warriors. Monks at Shaolin Monastery found the spears, which were originally intended for horseback fighting, too long for fighting on foot. They also found the aggressive-looking spearheads inappropriate in their peaceful monastic environment. So they removed the spearheads, and practised with only the shafts.

Shaolin disciples were, and still are, well known for their skills in using the staff. During the Tang Dynasty, a group of 500 monks from the monastery, used staffs to help the government quell a notorious bandit uprising. Later, when the Tang Dynasty itself became oppressive, a Shaolin disciple, Zhao Kuang Yin, used his staff – and of course also the soldiers who supported him – to found the Song Dynasty. If you are interested in the staff techniques this first Song emperor used, you can find them in a staff set known as Embracing Dragon Staff, although it is likely many of the original techniques would have been changed through time.

In one of his battles, it is said, a portion of the emperor's staff was cut off by an opposing general. The emperor must have been very sentimental about his staff, for instead of changing to a new staff, he joined the two portions with an iron chain. He then developed some very useful techniques with this new weapon, which he called a sweeper – presumably because he wanted to sweep away all his opponents with it. The sweeper became popular for some time: some people used it because it was effective, some because it was novel, and others because it was used by the emperor himself.

At that time carrying a weapon in public was not illegal. But while carrying a sweeper was allowed by law, it was nevertheless very inconvenient because it was a long weapon. Hence, some people shortened the shaft so that the two pieces could be placed together and tucked under clothing. This shortened weapon is called a small sweeper, to differentiate it from its longer brother, the big sweeper. You will probably recognize the small sweeper as the *nunchaku*, which is actually the Japanese pronunciation of the Chinese words meaning two-sectional staff, a name by which the small sweeper is also known.

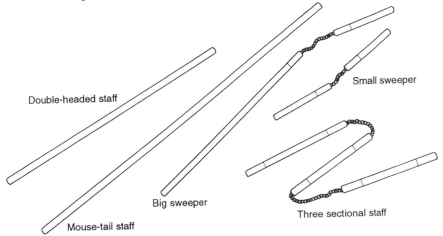

Fig 13.1 Various types of staffs

Although the two-sectional staff can be carried about conveniently, its combat functions are simple and few; thus it is not as effective as the big sweeper or other weapons. Although it was widely used in Japanese karate, it was not popular in Chinese Kung Fu. Recently, however, after the celebrated Bruce Lee introduced it into his films, it enjoyed an unprecedented spell of popularity. Some people, probably because of their lack of exposure to other, more elaborate weapons, even commented that it was an ingeniously efficient weapon. It became the fashion to use it, and even to hang it on walls as decoration.

Its cousin, the three-sectional staff, is more useful, with many and varied combat techniques. Because of its structure, it is comparatively difficult to learn to use it, but once the techniques are mastered, it becomes an exceedingly versatile weapon.

Whips, Knives and Other Weapons

There is another weapon with three sections, the three-sectional whip. A Chinese whip is very different from the conventional Western variety. The three-sectional whip consists of three short but heavy metal rods jointed together by chains, and attached to a handle. Using the three-sectional staff is difficult, but using the three-sectional whip is even more demanding. Some students have suggested wearing helmets in their practice, because if they are not careful their whips may hit their own heads, but that is not a good idea because it reflects poor control of the weapon. There are also five-, seven-, nine- and thirteen-sectional whips. These are referred to as soft whips, although the short steel rods of which they are comprised are very hard. They are called soft because they are flexible, and to distinguish them from the steel whip, which bears even less resemblance to a Western whip.

The steel whip is a piece of metal rod about 2½ft long, with ornamental bamboo-like designs on it. If it is plain, it is called a rod. A rod should be used as a rod and not as a knife or sword, because they have different combat properties. Like the steel whip or any heavy stick, a rod is mainly used for hitting, and if you want to stop an aggressor effectively without killing him or her, the best places to hit are the elbows, collar bones, knees and shins. A heavy strike on the head, however, can cause serious injury or even death.

With a rod you can smash your opponent if you strike hard, but to cut him or her into pieces — something you will be unlikely to want to do — you would need a blade weapon. There are many types of blade weapon

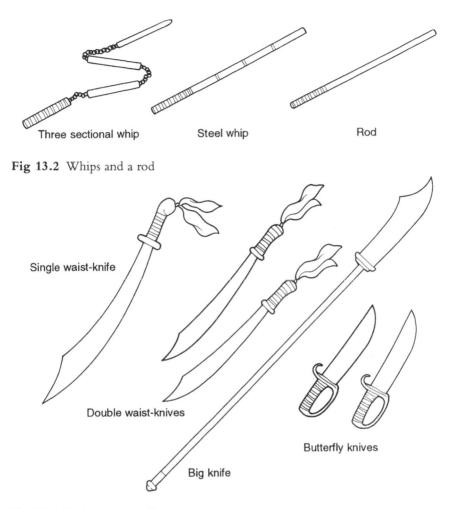

Three sectional whip   Steel whip   Rod

Fig 13.2 Whips and a rod

Single waist-knife

Double waist-knives

Big knife

Butterfly knives

Fig 13.3 Various types of knives

in Shaolin Kung Fu, and they are generally classified as knives. A Western reader would normally call them swords, using the term 'knives' for smaller utility implements. The Chinese, however, use 'swords' to denote double-bladed weapons which are usually light and dainty, and 'knives' for single-bladed weapons which are heavier and tougher. Knives and swords are qualitatively different – much more so than just in being single – or double-bladed. It is a sure sign that a person understands little about Kung Fu weapons if he or she uses a sword as if it were a knife.

There are three main categories of knives: the short butterfly knives, the intermediate waist knives, and the long big knives. Butterfly knives are about 1½ft long, and, like the wings of a butterfly, they are always used in pairs unless they are used in combination with other weapons.

Waist knives, which are about 3ft long, are often sheathed and worn at the waist. They are usually used singly, and are then known as single waist knives; but they are sometimes used in pairs, known as double waist knives. Western readers would probably associate a waist knife with a sabre or a scimitar.

Big knives are actually not big, but long – or rather their handles are long. The blade of a big knife is about 1½ft long, and is attached to a shaft measuring about 5ft. Probably the best known-exponent of the big knife was Guan Yi, a great general of the Three Kingdoms period (221–265 CE), who is honoured by the Chinese as the God of Righteousness, but often mistaken by the West as the God of War. So skilful was Guan Yi that the type of big knife that he used is now called the Guan *dao* or Guan knife. Other popular types of big knives are the nine-rings big knife, the block-the-gate big knife, and the chop-horse big knife.

Nine metal rings are attached to a nine-rings big knife so that a clanging sound is made when it is used. If you have guessed that the purpose of these noisy rings is to distract the opponent's attention, you are only partly right. When skilfully used, they can also hamper the opponent's weapon.

The block-the-gate big knife gets its name from its historical background. In ancient China bandit captains often used it to block any attack on the main gates of their hideouts, although of course not all those who used it were bandit captains. If you want to develop the skill to fight your way into bandits' hideouts to rescue damsels, you should familiarize yourself with this big knife! Know your opponent, including the weapon he uses, and you will win 100 times out of 100 battles – so advised Sun Tzu, one of the greatest strategists of ancient China.

Chop-horse big knives were not used by butchers for chopping meat off dead horses, but for soldiers chopping the legs off live ones, so that the warriors on the horses would fall from their horseback and be killed or captured. Unlike the other types of big knives, which were mainly used for horseback fighting, it was used for fighting on foot, especially against opponents on horseback. Thus, the shaft is shorter, and its blade longer than those of other big knives.

The Spear Family

The most popular weapon for horseback fighting throughout Chinese history has been the spear. This is understandable because technically it is easier and faster to pierce an opponent with a spear than to slash him with a blade weapon. There were numerous warriors in Chinese history noted

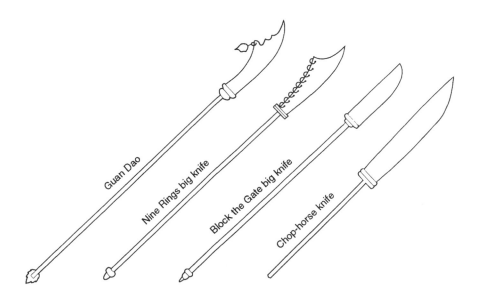

Fig 13.4 Various types of big knife

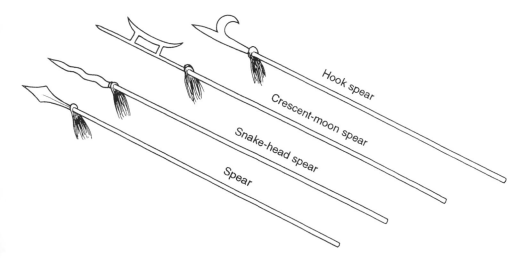

Fig 13.5 The spear family

for their excellence in using the spear, and some of the best known were the woman general Fan Li Hua of the Han Dynasty, the ever victorious Zhao Zi Long of the Three Kingdoms period, and the family of Yang generals of the Song Dynasty. So skilful was Zhao Zi Long with his spear that in his 50 years of military life he never lost a battle.

The spear has a head attached to a long shaft with a red tassel at the joint. There are some derivatives from the spear, such as the *mao*, or snake-headed spear, the *ji* or the crescent-moon spear and the hook spear.

The Three Kingdoms period, which was a time of heroic fighting and strategic manoeuvre, again supplies remarkable examples of famous masters using these weapons well. Zhang Dei, whose face was recorded as black like charcoal, and whose beard was as brittle as a brush, used a snake-headed spear 12ft long. Lu Bu, who was reputed to be as handsome as he was valiant, is perhaps the most famous exponent of the crescent-moon spear in Chinese history, and it is sometimes called Lu Bu *ji* after him.

The warrior who invented the hook spear was the great Song general Yue Fei, who was a Shaolin disciple. The Tartars who attacked the Song Dynasty were expert cavaliers, whereas the Song soldiers were mainly infantrymen. The Song army was no match at all against the Tartars, until Yue Fei, employing the principle of avoiding the opponents' strong points and attacking their weak ones, changed his soldiers' ordinary lances to hook spears to attack the legs of the enemies' horses, thus throwing the Tartars to the ground, where they became quite helpless.

Light and Heavy Weapons

An interesting contrast to the spear is the Chinese sword, which is always double-bladed with a pointed tip. It is therefore a weapon for thrusting as much as for slashing, but it is never used for hewing or chopping like a knife or an axe. Using a light, dainty sword as if it were a heavy, tough knife, swinging it round one's head and wielding it against an opponent's weapon, is a sure sign of someone who does not know how to use it properly.

A skilful swordsman tries to avoid clashing a sword with an opponent's heavy weapon, for doing so would blunt the razor-sharp edges, or break its delicate blade. A Chinese sword almost never touches an opponent's weapon during combat. Skilful dodging, precise anticipation and agility are necessary for good swordsmanship.

If one reduces the size of a sword, one has a dagger. But a dagger is used differently from a sword. The main combat function of a dagger is stabbing rather than thrusting, as with a sword, but if the opponent is very close, thrusting with a dagger can be a formidable technique. Learning to use a dagger to defend against an opponent with a longer weapon is a very useful way of developing the skill of dodging, which can be used in unarmed sparring.

If heavy and massive are the opposite of light and dainty, then the trident is the antithesis of the Chinese sword. While the sword is like a shy lady, the trident is like an insistent bully, always attempting to knock down the opponent's weapon by its massive weight. Sheer weight, however, is not its only asset. In the hands of a skilful exponent, its three heavy prongs can be used to lock or disarm an opponent.

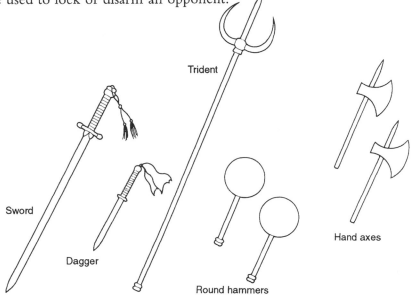

Fig 13.6 Light and heavy weapons

Moreover, it is more difficult for an opponent or a weapon to get past the three prongs of a trident and move along the shaft to strike the user than to get past the heads or the blades of other long weapons. There is also another interesting advantage in learning to use the trident. According to Chinese mythology, it is the most popular spiritual weapon for chasing away, or keeping under control, evil spirits. So, by practising with this weapon, you may acquire some of this aura.

Another heavy weapon is the round hammer. This is a short weapon, and is usually used in pairs, each hand holding one hammer. It is an ancient weapon, which was popular in the Shang (1520–1030 BCE) and Zhou (1030–480 BCE) Dynasties, when copper was often used to cast it. It is therefore often called the copper hammer, although it may be made from other materials. It became less popular later because people had devised other, less clumsy and more effective, weapons. Nevertheless, if you practise a round hammer set nowadays, you will find it a useful way to develop stamina and power.

Another short, heavy weapon normally used in pairs is the hand axe. It is sometimes called the whirlwind axe, because a skilful exponent can create a little whirlwind by swinging it vigorously. The hand axe originated from the ancient long battle axe, which was widely used in horseback fighting during the early Chinese dynasties. It was later displaced by the big knife, and then the long spear.

Common Implements as Weapons

While some weapons like the battle axe and the crescent-moon spear are exotic, others are more commonplace – items in normal circumstances which can be used as weapons in times of need. The umbrella, the bench and the walking stick are some examples of these implement-weapons.

The Chinese bench, which was frequently used in tea houses in classical China, is still a common feature in many Eastern countries today. The umbrella and the walking stick are very useful weapons if one knows how to use them as such. If you do not normally use a walking stick – and of course one aim of Kung Fu training is to help you do without one as you get older – learning a set of umbrella techniques may one day prove to be very useful in self-defence.

You should not, however, use an umbrella the way a lady in a comic strip would use it, by hitting an assailant on the head with it. If you do, it will usually be the umbrella not the head that breaks. The potentially destructive property of an umbrella is in its pointed end. An umbrella in combat, therefore, is more advantageously used for thrusting than for hitting. Should you need to hit with it, use the hard handle instead of the cushioned ribs.

This illustrates two important points that may save your life one day. Improvized weapons for self-defence are all around if you look for them, and you should use their destructive properties if you want them to be effective. For example if an assailant attacks you with a knife or a dagger, do not fight back empty-handed or worse still just stand there helplessly. Quickly grab a chair or stool, and simultaneously shout for help. Your shouting may attract others to your aid, and it may also frighten the assailant into running away.

You should hold the chair or stool in such a way that its legs point towards the assailant. If he or she still threatens you, do not just stand and wait. Take the initiative and strike first. Do not strike the head or body, because while you are doing so he or she may thrust the weapon at you. Use the legs of the chair to strike the hand that is holding the weapon; it is like four rods striking at the same time. If you hit hard enough, he or she may drop the weapon. If you get the arm between the legs of the chair, turn it round so that the legs twist it. Having disarmed the assailant, and if you are fighting for your life, thrust a leg of the chair right into the face. Then the assailant will either run away, or hold his or her face in pain. You can pick up the weapon and run away, shouting for help and still holding the chair just in case the assailant chases you.

14

UNDERSTANDING AND DEVELOPING CHI

The Philosophy and Methods of Shaolin Chi Kung

❖ *The key to all the achievements that distinguish Shaolin Kung Fu from other martial arts is Shaolin Chi Kung.*

From Combat Efficiency to Spiritual Development

There are many reasons why Shaolin Kung Fu is considered by many as the greatest martial art in the world. One reason is the great variety of techniques, which are not only effective for combat but also artistic to watch. Another is its fantastic internal force, which does not depend on brute strength, and which does not diminish with age. The third reason is that Shaolin Kung Fu training helps students to be emotionally calm and mentally fresh, whereas some martial arts training makes the students aggressive and stressful.

Fourthly, Shaolin Kung Fu promotes health and longevity, while some martial arts are detrimental to health and adversely affect their students by damaging the physiological functions of their hands, legs and other parts of the body through hard conditioning, and by causing injury in sparring practice without taking appropriate measures to prevent or cure it.

However, the most important reason why Shaolin Kung Fu can claim to be the greatest martial art is that it leads to the highest spiritual fulfilment, the greatest attainment any person can ever achieve, irrespective of race, culture or religion, or indeed even when the exponent professes no religion. The key to all the achievements that distinguish Shaolin Kung Fu from other martial arts is Shaolin Chi Kung, which will be explained in this chapter.

Those who think of martial arts as merely tough training for fighting may have difficulty accepting such claims. It is a fundamental tenet of Shaolin teaching, like the Buddha's teaching from which it draws its inspiration and which Shaolin Monastery was built to promote, that one should not accept any teaching on faith alone or on the reputation of masters but, after practising the teaching diligently with an open mind, to assess it to the best of our understanding and experience. And the benefits of the training methods described in this book are substantiated by my students' and my own experience. Moreover, the other Shaolin arts mentioned but not described in detail are taken from established authoritative texts.

If you have been practising Shaolin Kung Fu for many years but have never experienced these benefits, it would be advisable to review what went wrong by referring to the Three Requirements for Attainment discussed in Chapter 5. Shaolin Chi Kung is the key to all these benefits, so if you have not practised Shaolin Chi Kung adequately – which would not be surprising as until recently it was reserved only for selected disciples – that may be the main reason why you have not got the most from your Shaolin Kung Fu training.

Chi Kung, spelt *qigong* in Romanized Chinese, is the umbrella term for the arts of developing vital energy.[1] There are literally hundreds of types, most of which consist of only a narrow range of techniques with limited objectives.

Shaolin Chi Kung is a very large family containing a wide variety of types and an extensive range of objectives. At one end of the spectrum are exercises for the weak, the old and the sick to regain their health, while at the other end, at the highest level, are exercises for spiritual development. Much of what lies in between is aimed at developing power and stamina for combat efficiency. The variation from the elementary to the advanced lies not only in the techniques used, but also in the skills developed. The same exercise, for example, may be used by a sick person to recover from illness, or by a radiantly healthy master to deepen spirituality.

The Various Genres of Chi Kung

The types of exercise contained in all the schools of Chi Kung may be classified into four categories: Dynamic Patterns, Self-Manifested Chi Movement, Quiescent Breathing and Silent Sitting. While many types or schools are concerned mainly with one category, all four are found in Shaolin Chi Kung.

This classification is intended to help one's understanding and the attainment of objectives, and is not meant to be restrictive. Hence, the categories sometimes overlap. Examples of the first three categories are discussed in this chapter; the fourth category will be described in some detail in the next.

The category of Dynamic Patterns refers to a genre of Chi Kung exercises where external physical movements are used to generate internal energy flow. At a higher level of skill, visualization is employed. The well known set of eight exercises known as *ba duan jin*, meaning 'Eight Pieces of Brocade', which coincide with the first eight exercises in the Eighteen Lohan Hands practised in our Shaolin Wahnam School, provides a good example of eight Dynamic Patterns.

In Self-Manifested Chi Movement, or *zi fa dong gong* practitioners induce chi or energy to move inside their bodies, and may move about involuntarily, sometimes in an extraordinary way! This may seem hard to believe, but you will have a chance to experience it yourself in a Self-Manifested Chi Kung exercise which is explained later in this chapter. This form of Chi Kung is also called Self-Induced Chi Flow, and probably the most famous example is *wu qin xi* or Five Animals Play, which was taught by the famous 3rd century Chinese physician Hua Tuo, considered by many as the saint of Chinese medicine.

Quiescent Breathing, known in Chinese as *lian qi*, meaning 'training energy,' or *tiao xi*, meaning 'regulating breath', refers to exercises where the practitioners usually stand, but sometimes sit, motionlessly focusing on various methods of breath control. This important state is often described by Chi Kung masters as 'external quiescence, internal dynamism', meaning that there is little or no visible external movement, but perceptible harmonious energy flow inside the body. Some people, incorrectly but not without some justification, refer to Quiescent Breathing as the most typical of Chi Kung types. The best example is probably Abdominal Breathing, which we shall study later in this chapter, because it forms the basis of all types of Chi Kung breathing.

Silent Sitting or *jing zuo*, the fourth genre, refers to meditation in a sitting position, especially in the lotus position, where the emphasis is on chi training rather than on mind training. The distinction between chi and mind training, as well as that between Silent Sitting for chi training and Quiescent Breathing, is slight and arbitrary.

In Silent Sitting, practitioners may not deliberately breathe in cosmic energy through the nose, but by using the mind they can tap a lot more cosmic energy through their bodies than by breathing through their noses. The Small Universe or Microcosmic Flow of Taoist Chi Kung, where the mind rather than breathing is used to direct vital energy round the body, is a good example of Silent Sitting.

The Three Elements of Chi Kung

Just as in Kung Fu, so in Chi Kung training, some basic theoretical knowledge will help us greatly, not only in getting better results more quickly, but in achieving the best possible results the particular exercises are designed to give. Indeed, most people derive only a small portion of the benefits that Chi Kung can provide, because they lack the basic Chi Kung knowledge.

All the different kinds of Chi Kung exercises can be grouped into three elements, known in Chinese as body, breath and heart, which can be translated as the form aspect, the energy aspect, and the mind aspect. In the past, many masters referred to Chi Kung training as *san tiao*, or the Three Regulations: regulating the body, which will promote health and fitness; regulating the breath, which will result in the increase and the harmonious flow of vital energy in the body; and regulating the 'heart', which means mind control and expansion.

Hence, students who merely practise the physical movements of a Chi Kung exercise, as many do, without realizing its energy and mind aspects, will derive at best only a small portion of the potential benefits – less than one third, because although form is one of the three aspects of Chi Kung, it is the least important. It is significant to note that Chi Kung is basically an internal art; practising it without its internal aspects of energy and mind is degrading it into just a form of gentle exercise.

From the perspective of health, if our chi or vital energy is adequate and flows harmoniously in our body, we will be fit and healthy. This may seem a simple statement, but it is the most fundamental principle of Chinese medicine, the system of health care that has successfully served the largest population of the world with the longest continuous civilization in history. All forms of Chinese medical practice, such as herbalism, massage therapy, acupuncture, Chi Kung therapy and tranatology (a unique form of Chinese medicine closely related to Kung Fu, specializing in treating injury rather than illness), are practical means of effecting a harmonious flow of chi in the patient.

Expressing the same concept in Western medical terms may not be appropriate because Western medicine uses a different paradigm, but we may obtain a fairly good idea of this crucial Chinese concept by saying in Western terms that if the feedback system, self-defence system, immune system, self-generative system, hormonal system, digestive system, transportation system, excretory system and other crucial body systems are restored to their natural functions, the patient will be restored to health.

This is a great universal truth; we are by nature healthy; illness is an unnatural, temporary state when certain systems of the body are not functioning as they should. The harmonious flow of chi restores a person's natural functions. It is also excellent for overcoming emotional and mental problems and managing stress.

From the perspective of Kung Fu, which requires health as a prerequisite, the harmonious flow of chi serves many functions, such as enabling the exponent to channel intrinsic energy to wherever it is needed as internal force, ensuring a constant supply of energy for better stamina, cleansing the body of injuries sustained during training or sparring, and circulating round the body like a protective cushion against an opponent's attack. If students are not healthy, they should practise Chi Kung to restore their health before attempting serious Kung Fu.

Besides promoting a more harmonious flow of vital energy, a Chi Kung practitioner also increases the amount of vital energy by tapping it from the Cosmos and storing it at the abdominal *dan tian* or the energy field known as *qi-hai*. There are also other important *dan tian* or energy fields, such as *bai-hui* at the crown of the head, *tian-mu* at the third eye, *tan-zhong* at the solar plexus, *min-men* at the waist between the kidneys, *hui-yin* at the bottom of the body between the genitals and the anus, *lao-gong* at the centres of the palms, and *yong-quan* at the soles of the feet.

In Chi Kung terms, energy in the open is generally referred to as *tian qi*, or 'heaven energy', translated here as cosmic energy; energy derived from food and drinks is called *di qi*, or 'earth energy'; energy inside the body, which is essential for life functions, and which for most people is the result of the interaction of heaven energy and earth energy is known as *zhen qi*, or 'real energy', translated here as vital energy.

From Chi Kung training we can obtain vital energy directly from cosmic energy. So, without knowing how to tap cosmic energy and to direct the energy flow, a student will miss out on a crucial part of Chi Kung training.

Vital energy may be increased and made to flow by means of appropriate physical exercises, but the effect is incidental and minimal. The best approach is to use the mind, but the mind has to be tamed and trained before it will follow one's bidding. The Buddha said an untrained mind is like a monkey, always restless and never still, even for a moment. Some masters believe that your mind is the real you. We need not debate here whether the real you and your mind are the actually same; you can investigate that question in Zen training in the next chapter.

Shaolin Kung Fu training and Shaolin Chi Kung training incorporate some excellent methods for taming and training the mind. That is the reason why many of my students who have practised different forms of meditation before but with little result, suddenly find that their meditation improves after Kung Fu or Chi Kung training. The benefit is mutual; a trained mind also enhances the benefits of Kung Fu and Chi Kung training. The trained mind is focused, clear and tranquil; then it expands and eventually leads to spiritual fulfilment, which will be explained in the next chapter. Thus, a student with many years of Kung Fu or Chi Kung training who has not understood and practised this mind aspect and therefore cannot use the mind to accumulate and channel intrinsic energy, is not likely to reach a very high level.

Advanced Chi Kung training should be done with the personal supervision of a master or at least a competent instructor. However, if you cannot find an instructor, you may attempt the first two exercises in this chapter on your own, but do not pay too much attention to visualization. If you have some experience in Kung Fu or Chi Kung, you may try the third exercise, on Abdominal Breathing, but you must be careful to progress slowly and gradually, and you must supplement your training with the first two exercises at least once every three days as a safeguard to cleanse away any harmful side effects that you may unwittingly develop. If you are a beginner, it is not advisable to attempt Abdominal Breathing.

Lifting the Sky

This is one of the best Dynamic Patterns in all schools of Chi Kung. It is simple, yet the benefits are fantastic. It can be appreciated at different levels: beginners as well as masters can enjoy the same exercises with different benefits according to their needs and abilities.

1 Stand upright and relax, with your feet fairly close together. Place both palms in front of you with the fingers closed and pointing together, the open palms facing downward, and the elbows straight.
2 Without moving your body, tilt your head to look at your palms — *figure 14.1 (a)*.
3 Then move both palms, with elbows straight, in a continuous arc forwards and upwards until they are above you with the open palms facing the sky, simultaneously breathing in gently through your nose, and following your hand movement with your eyes — *figure 14.1 (b)*.
4 Stop breathing and moving for a second or two, then press up with your palms against the sky.

5 Then gently straighten your body and head, and lower your arms to your sides, with the elbows still straight, breathing out through your mouth at the same time – *figure 14.1 (c)*.
6 Stop breathing and moving for two or three seconds when your arms are at your sides – *figure 14.1 (d)*.
7 Repeat the whole procedure about 10–20 times.
8 At the end of the exercise, remain in the standing meditation position for 5–10 minutes, and end by rubbing your palms, warming your eyes with them as you open your eyes, and walking about briskly as in the standard procedure for completing an exercise involving meditation.

Fig 14.1 Lifting the Sky

After you have practised Lifting the Sky at least once daily for a few weeks, when you can co-ordinate your breathing with your movement with ease, you may attempt the mind aspect of this exercise. As you breathe in when you raise your arms, visualize good cosmic energy flowing into you. As you breathe out when you lower your arms, visualize the energy flowing through your whole body from your head right down to the soles of your feet, cleansing away toxic waste, illness, negative emotions or any rubbish that you do not want. If you are an environmentalist, take comfort in the fact that the negativity cleansed out of your body can be beneficial to other things or beings in the ground.

The visualization must be performed very gently, and do not attempt it unless you can perform the physical and breathing aspects of the exercise well.

Lohan Embracing Buddha

This is a wonderful exercise which generates harmonious energy flow, thereby relieving illness and injury and promoting health. If you have not heard of or seen Self-Manifested Chi Movement before, you may think it is impossible, but it has been practised for a very long time, although until recently it was preserved as a carefully guarded secret.

Before attempting Self-Manifested Chi Movement, you should know a few things. If you perform the exercise correctly, you may move involuntarily. Generally this takes the form of gentle swaying, but for some people the movements may be vigorous, and they may make funny noises. These are the natural results of your relaxed reaction to enhanced flow of vital energy inside your body.

You should not resist if you feel your vital energy moving your body; just follow the momentum and enjoy it. But at the early stage, when you have not perfected your control over the exercise, if your movements begin to be too vigorous, you should relax and mentally tell your movements to slow down. You will be surprised that you have this ability of mind over matter. Never stop abruptly, even if someone visits you or your telephone rings; always bring your movement to a graceful stop. Make sure that your training place is safe, away from balconies, high windows or sharp objects.

The Self-Manifested Chi Movement exercise below is named after the first pattern, Lohan Embracing Buddha, for easy reference. Perform each of the three patterns about 20 times. The 60 patterns should be performed without break, as if they were one long, continuous pattern. Let your breathing be spontaneous, and your mind empty of all thoughts throughout the exercise.

1 Stand upright and relax. Men should place the left middle finger and women the right middle finger on the navel and press gently about 10 times.
2 Drop the finger and place the other middle finger on the crown of the head and massage it about three times.
3 Then place both arms in front of you, with the elbows bent slightly, the palms facing inwards and the fingers pointing towards one another, as if you were holding a big barrel. The pattern is called Lohan Embracing Buddha.
4 Without moving your feet, but relaxing your knees, turn your body from left to right about 20 times, each turn from one side to another counting as one time – *figure 14.2 (a)*.

5 Next place your right hand above your head with your right palm facing upwards, your right elbow bent and your right fingers pointing towards your left. Place your left hand near your left thigh, your left palm facing downwards, your left elbow almost straight, and your left fingers pointing towards your left. Look at your left hand and shift your weight over your right leg – *figure 14.2 (b)*. This pattern is called Dancing Fairies.

6 Shift your weight from your right to your left leg, and simultaneously move your left hand up and your right hand down, and turn to look at your right hand – *figure 14.2 (c)*.

7 Repeat about 20 times, each shift counting as one time.

8 Spread out both arms at shoulder level, elbows straight, palms facing downwards and fingers pointing outwards. Turn to your left and kick

(a)   (b)   (c)

(d)   (e)

Fig 14.2 Lohan Embracing Buddha

up at your left palm with your right foot – *figure 14.2 (d)*. Then turn to your right and kick up at your right palm with your left foot – *figure 14.2 (e)*. Your arms should be held straight at shoulder level throughout. This pattern is called Lohan Kicking Oranges.

9   Repeat about 20 times, each kick counting as one time.
10   After performing the 60 patterns continuously, drop your arms at your sides, stand upright, close your eyes gently and relax. When you feel that you are being moved by your internal chi flow, do not resist the movement but follow the momentum. Soon you will enjoy Self-Manifested Chi Movement. Keep your eyes gently closed and your mind empty of all thoughts.
11   After about 10 minutes of Self-Manifested Chi Movement, or whenever you have had enough of the exercise, gently but firmly tell your movement to slow down then eventually stop. Keep still for a few minutes, and gently think of your abdomen. Then complete the exercise using the standard procedure described above.

You will probably find this Chi Kung exercise one of the most memorable experiences of your life.

Abdominal Breathing

You are recommended to practise this breathing exercise under the supervision of a competent instructor. Beginners are advised not to attempt it on their own, as they may hurt themselves unwittingly if they practise incorrectly.

1   Stand upright with your feet fairly close together and relax. You may closes or open your eyes for this exercise.
2   Place one palm on your abdominal energy field (about 3in below your navel) and the other palm on top of it. Press down on your abdomen with both palms gently and smoothly for about six counts. Breathe naturally, but make sure that you do not breathe in as you press on your abdomen. Hold for about two counts.
3   Then gently and smoothly release the pressure of your palms on your abdomen in about six counts so that the abdomen rises to its original position.
4   Pause for about two counts. Repeat about 10 times.
5   Drop your arms to your sides, close your eyes (if they are not already closed) and remain in the standing meditation position for a few minutes. Finish by using the standard procedure.

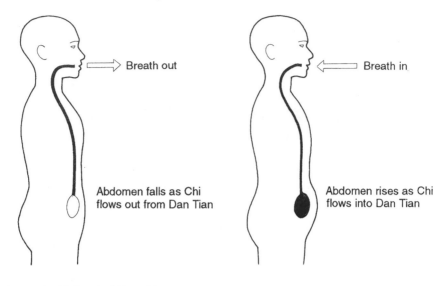

Fig 14.3 Abdominal Breathing

Practise the above exercise for at least two weeks. Gradually increase the number of times you press and release the abdomen to about 36. Then proceed to the second stage.

The method for the second stage is the same as that for the first, except that as you press your abdomen, visualize that all the toxic waste, illness, negative emotions and other unwanted things are flowing out through your mouth. As you release the presure, visualize good cosmic energy flowing through your nose and into your abdomen. You need not worry about your breathing at this stage. Practise for at least two weeks before proceeding to the next stage.

In the third stage, practise as for the second stage except that as you press your abdomen, breathe out gently through your mouth, with your negative energy flowing out. As you release your pressure and your abdomen rises, breathe in good cosmic energy gently through your nose, and let the energy accumulate at your abdominal *dan tian*. Be gentle both in breathing in and breathing out.

You may reach a very deep level of meditation while practising Abdominal Breathing. During your standing meditation, gently think of your abdomen. Gradually you will feel a ball of energy at your abdomen. If you practise daily for at least six months, you will find yourself radiating health and vitality.

15

SHAOLIN KUNG FU
AND ZEN

The Study of Ultimate Reality and Phenomenal World

❖ *We shall address ourselves to the question of what ultimate reality is, and its related question of why the so-called external, objective world is an illusion.*

Cultivating Heart, Nourishing Nature

The master who introduced me to my lifelong love of the Shaolin arts was my first Kung Fu teacher, Uncle Righteousness, a highly respected Shaolin master. Uncle Righteousness was the honourable nickname by which Kung Fu circles in particular and the public in general addressed my master; his real name was Lai Chin Wah. One of the best lessons I learned from him was that the highest Kung Fu is what is known in Chinese as *xiu xin yang xing*, which literally means 'cultivate heart, nourish nature'.

I was too young at that time, to appreciate fully the real meaning of 'cultivate heart, nourish nature'. It was much later that I had the rare opportunity to practise it with another Shaolin master, Sifu Ho Fatt Nam, who was directly descended from the Southern Shaolin Monastery. From Sifu Ho, I learned another very important lesson. He told me:

> If you want to soar to the heights and reach the depths of Kung Fu, you must practise Chi Kung; if you want to soar to the heights and reach the depths of Chi Kung, you must practise meditation.

Shaolin meditation is Zen, which involves 'cultivating heart, nourishing nature'.

To most people, this means developing a noble character and amiable disposition. But this is only the first step in Shaolin Kung Fu, not its highest achievement. In Chinese, 'heart' usually refers to what the West would call 'mind', and 'nature' here means 'Buddha nature'. Hence, 'cultivate heart, nourish nature' actually means cultivate your mind, which is the same as the Universal Mind, and nourish your nature which is the same as Buddha nature. This was exactly what the great Bodhidharma, the first Patriarch of the Shaolin arts, wanted his disciples to achieve when he taught at Shaolin Monastery in the early 6th century.

In Buddhist terms this is seeking enlightenment, ie cultivating our mind so that we realize our mind is the Universal Mind, and nourishing our nature so that we realize our nature is actually the Buddha nature.

But what is meant by Universal Mind and Buddha nature? These are Zen terms referring to the Ultimate Truth or the Supreme Reality. In other religious terms, it is the same as returning to God, union with Brahman or merging with the Cosmos.

Zen, here, is a shortened form of Zen Buddhism, which is a major school of Mahayana Buddhism. Buddhism is the teachings of the Buddhas, or Enlightened Ones. There have been, and will be, countless Buddhas, not only in our world but also in countless other worlds and galaxies. While orthodox scientists still believe that life exists only in our puny world, an infinitesimal speck in the known universe, Buddhists believe that life is everywhere, and in more forms than ordinary minds can conceive. The Buddha of our world in our aeon is Sakyamuni Buddha (also called Gautama Buddha), who is normally referred to as the Buddha. The Buddha of our previous aeon was Kasyapa Buddha, and of our coming aeon will be Maitreya Buddha. There are at present also Buddhas in other worlds in other stars, such as Amitabha Buddha in a distant galaxy in the west, and Askhobhya Buddha in the east.

Buddhism is not a religion in the sense in which most Westerners use the word. Indeed terms like 'Buddhism' and 'Buddhists' are labels given by the West for the purpose of identification and differentiation. In Eastern societies people since ancient times have been practising the teachings of the Enlightened Ones without being aware that they were Buddhists. That is why the Chinese, as well as other peoples, can be Buddhist, Taoist and Confucianist all at the same time. That was also why people of different religions practised the Shaolin arts, including Zen Buddhism, in Shaolin Monastery.

Discipline and Wisdom

There are two main traditions in Buddhism, Theravada and Mahayana. Theravada Buddhism, which flourishes in Sri Lanka, Myanmar (Burma), Thailand and Cambodia, is often referred to as Buddhism of the Elders because the Council of Senior Monks played a significant role in its development. Mahayana Buddhism, which is widespread in China, Japan, Korea, Vietnam, Malaysia and Singapore, is often referred to as Buddhism of the Great Vehicle because of its emphasis on universal enlightenment and not just personal salvation. Vajrayana Buddhism, called Buddhism of the Diamond Vehicle because of its many facets, which is popular in Tibet, Mongolia and Nepal, developed from Mahayana Buddhism, but is now often referred to as the third Buddhist tradition.

The differences between the three Buddhist traditions are mainly developmental and cultural; they all have the same basic teaching and the same ultimate aim. The basic teaching can be best summed up in the Buddha's own words:

> Avoid all evil,
> Do good,
> Purify the mind.

The ultimate aim of Buddhism is to attain enlightenment. In the Buddhist context, enlightenment means something vastly different from the Western concept, as in the Age of Enlightenment, which implies an intellectual understanding of processes or events. In Buddhism, the most important aspect in any attainment is direct experience, not intellectual understanding. In other words, it is not enough merely to understand what enlightenment is, although that is helpful; it must be experienced if it is to constitute any attainment. We will discuss enlightenment in detail later, but meanwhile let us briefly study the three features of the Buddha's basic teaching.

A very useful guide, to help anyone of any religion to avoid evil is to follow the five basic precepts of Buddhism, the teachings of the Enlightened Ones:

- no killing
- no stealing
- no lying
- no sexual misconduct
- no intoxication (because it dulls the mind)

Some readers who are used to the concept of positive thinking may think the five precepts negative because they stress not doing evil rather than doing good. Three points are relevant here. First, Buddhists do also stress doing good. Secondly, not doing evil is not the same as doing good. Thirdly, one should cultivate the more basic tenet of not doing evil before focusing on doing good. Hence, a rich man may contribute handsomely to charity, but if he has earned his wealth through dishonest means, his 'doing good' would lose its significance.

Doing good includes doing good to others as well as to oneself. The following six *paramitas*, which constitute a fundamental training programme in Mahayana Buddhism, provide guidance to those who wish to do good:

- charity
- morality
- tolerance
- perseverance
- meditation
- wisdom

The first three concern doing good to others, whereas the last three concern doing good to oneself. This is typical of Mahayana philosophy, ie helping others is as important as helping ourselves.

It is a misconception to think that one needs a lot of money to be charitable. According to the Buddha's teaching, there are three levels of charity. The lowest is the giving of money and material goods, the second is the giving of service and the highest is the giving of teaching, especially religious or spiritual teaching. Hence, if you take the trouble to stop your car to help a blind man cross a road, you are probably being more charitable than a rich man giving money to a blind charity.

The purpose of purifying the mind, the third aspect of the basic teaching in the Buddha's own words, is to attain enlightenment, which is achieved through the triple training process of discipline, meditation and wisdom. In the six *paramitas*, discipline comprises the first four and meditation and wisdom the last two. In the Eightfold Path, a fundamental training process in Theravada Buddhism, discipline comprises right thought, right speech, right conduct, right livelihood and right effort; meditation comprises right concentration and right mindfulness; and wisdom comprises right understanding. While cultivating discipline is a continuous process, it is also the prerequisite for mind purification, which is attained through meditation. Meditation will lead to wisdom, especially the wisdom regarding the realization of ultimate reality.

The wisdom found in Buddhist teaching is awe-inspiring. Buddhist wisdom, originally acquired through meditation where different aspects of reality are directly perceived, is recorded in the huge body of Buddhist scriptures collectively known as the Tripitaka, which is the largest collection of religious works in the world, consisting of over 7000 volumes. It comprises three sections: *sutras*, which are the teachings of the Buddha in his own words; *vinaya*, which is a collection of monastic rules and related stories; and *sastras*, which are treaties and commentaries written by Buddhist masters.

If you imagine that these extensive volumes of Buddhist scriptures involve persuasion and moralization, teaching people to be pious or religious, you are mistaken. The scriptures explain, if you can understand its classical language and profound concepts, ideas that physicists, cosmologists, psychologists and other scientists and philosophers are currently investigating, such as time and space, matter and energy, subatomic activities, the multi-dimensional universe, shadow matter, and different levels of consciousness. This is not surprising if we remember that Buddhism, like science and philosophy, investigates what reality is. It is beyond the scope of this book to describe in detail the Buddhist wisdom regarding these aspects of reality, but we shall address ourselves to the question of what ultimate reality is, and its related question of why the so-called external objective world is an illusion, as such an understanding is relevant to the highest attainment of Shaolin Kung Fu.

What is Ultimate Reality?

The following theme line from the well-known but little understood *Heart Sutra*, one of the most important and beautiful works in Buddhism, serves as a good introduction to cosmic reality:

> Form is emptiness; and emptiness is form.

Many people will find this line puzzling. They are equally bewildered by basic Buddhist teachings such as that the phenomenal world is an illusion, and ultimate reality is tranquil and undifferentiated. Interestingly, modern science provides a clear explanation for this Buddhist teaching.

In our ordinary consciousness, an opponent is real. If he or she attacks you and if you fail to defend yourself there is no illusion about your being hit. But suppose we look at the same situation from the very high level of consciousness of an enlightened being like a Buddha or a Bodhisattva who sees reality as it ultimately is and not as it is grossly modified by a set of conditions. You may not have reached the level of a Bodhisattva, but here is where modern science can help us. Suppose you were able to look through a gigantic, super-powerful electron microscope. What would you see? Your opponent would have disappeared! What you thought was the form of a person would turn out to be almost emptiness; you would see patterns of subatomic particles as far apart as specks of stars in outer space. If you looked at yourself you would be equally astonished; your body too would have disappeared!

If the microscope were more powerful, like the wisdom-eye of a Bodhisattva, you would realize that the so-called subatomic particles are actually not particles; they are concentrations of energy without any definite boundary. You may be reminded of Neil Bohr's Principle of Complementarity – that an electron can be a wave or a particle.

But more importantly, you would suddenly be awakened to the great cosmic truth that as there is no boundary separating one subatomic particle from another, there is also no boundary separating you from your opponent or anything else. In other words, the whole universe is actually a continuous spread of energy or consciousness, without any differentiation. You would be awakened to the greatest truth of all – the discovery that great masters of all religions and mystical disciplines have made – that the physical body in which, owing to your ignorance, you have imprisoned yourself, is an illusion, and that your personal mind is actually the Universal Mind. This feeling of liberation gives us tremendous calm and blessedness. The ecstatic exclamations of great masters such as 'I dissolve myself in the infinite grace of God', 'There is no difference between the Cosmos and me', and 'My own nature is the Buddha nature' become meaningful.

This is Zen, which in this context means a glimpse of cosmic reality in its transcendental aspect, and which is called *wu* in Chinese and *kensho* or *satori* in Japanese, and is best translated as 'awakening' in English. An awakening is not enlightenment; it is nevertheless a confirmation that you are on the way to enlightenment if you persist in your cultivation. Awakening is a cosmic glimpse, whereas enlightenment is a total, direct becoming of the Cosmos, where all dualism disappears, where there is no difference between the knower and the known. When you attain enlightenment, you are not extinguished, as is sometimes misconceived; you become – are – the Cosmos. What endeavour can be grander, more noble than cultivating this attainment? Enlightenment is called by various names in Buddhism, such as *nirvana, bodhi,* Buddhahood and Zen.

Zen, therefore, has a few related meanings. It can mean both a cosmic glimpse and the total cosmic realization. It can also refer to meditation, the essential way to both the cosmic glimpse and the cosmic realization. It is also a shortened form for Zen Buddhism, the school of Buddhism especially devoted to the attainment of Zen in all its three meanings.

After you have come out of Zen, you may ask whether your opponent, you or anything else is real. The Zen answer is yes and no, either yes or no, neither yes nor no. If you think this is crazy, be assured that sensible, serious scientists today would give similar answers if you ask them whether a virtual particle, or a 'real' particle like a photon or an electron, or even a tangible object like a cat, or a huge heavenly body like the moon, really exists. After the scientific revolution brought about by such great scientists as Einstein, Max Planck, Neil Bohr and Werner Heisenberg, modern scientists have accepted, many centuries after the Buddha, that our so-called objective external world is actually a creation of the mind. The American physicist, Professor David Mermim, has seriously declared that 'we now know the moon is demonstrably not there when nobody looks'.[1]

When Buddhist masters say that the external world is an illusion, they do not mean that it is imaginary, but that it is only relatively, not absolutely, real. A bacterium inside your opponent, or a sentient being from another realm of existence, will see that person very differently from the way you do, because you, the bacterium and the extraterrestrial being experience him or her under different conditions. Even if you slightly change your conditions, such as wearing a pair of glasses with strange lenses, the same opponent will appear differently. But if you, the bacterium and the extraterrestrial being were enlightened, or at least awakened, you would all see things the same way, for all would have perceived ultimate reality, ie cosmic reality without any conditions.

What is ultimate reality like? Masters of all religions and mystical disciplines have insisted that it is inexplicable. This does not mean that they did not want to tell people, or that they themselves did not know. But if you want to know what it is, you have to experience it yourself, just as in Shaolin Kung Fu, if you want to know what internal force is you have to acquire it to find out. In a simpler, more prosaic example, if you want to know the taste of a mango, you have to taste it; no amount of description can exactly convey its taste to you. Yet, to help people, to give them some, albeit imperfect idea of ultimate reality, Buddhist masters have described it as tranquil, undifferentiated and void.

The word 'void' may be misleading. Void or emptiness, known as *sunyata* in Sanskrit and *kong* in Chinese, which is the hallmark of Mahayana teaching, does not mean absolute nothingness; it means devoid or emptied of phenomena or appearances. Hence, phenomena like houses, cars, trees, the sky, the moon and stars are appearances; they are not ultimately real. Their appearances depend on a set of conditions, such as the range of light the observer is able to see, and the way each person's consciousness as well as the collective consciousness of the group are accustomed to operate. If conditions change, the appearances change. For example, instead of viewing the sky in our ordinary light, a Harvard astronomer viewed it using ultra-violet rays; he found not one but three suns, and the moon almost disappeared.[2]

Bodhidharma and Taoism in Zen

Investigating the nature of reality is an important feature of mind development in the highest Shaolin Kung Fu, which is Zen cultivation. Zen was transmitted from India to China by Bodhidharma, who like the Buddha before him renounced his luxurious life as a prince to seek and attain enlightenment. Some scholars who have probably never practised Zen, but may have spent a few years reading about it, often from secondary sources, claim that Bodhidharma was a myth, and Zen Buddhism was a Chinese invention based on Taoism. But Zen masters of all nationalities, including all the great Chinese masters, gratefully honour Bodhidharma as the first Patriarch for initiating Zen in China, where it blossomed and spread to Japan, Korea, Vietnam and other countries.

The evidence for Bodhidharma's residence in China is overwhelming. Imperial records mention his arrival at Canton, southern China around 520 CE, his interview with Emperor Liang Wu Di, when he told the emperor that the first principle in Buddhism is emptiness not holiness, and his teaching at Shaolin Monastery about 527. The pavilion named after Bodhidharma is in the main building of Shaolin Monastery, the First Patriarch Temple built in his honour still stands in the extensive monastery complex some distance from the main building, and the cave behind the building where he meditated for nine years is still called Bodhidharma Cave. All established Zen masters traced their genealogical lines, which are surprisingly well kept despite their long history, back to Bodhidharma.

Those who claim that Zen Buddhism originated from Taoism are mainly either Chinese Confucian scholars of literature who have practised neither Zen nor Taoism deeply, or Western scholars who base their opinion on superficial Chinese sources. A deeper study of Taoism and Zen will show that their approaches to the realization of ultimate reality are basically different, and an investigation of the history of Zen development in China will show little Taoist influence. As my master, Sifu Ho Fatt Nam, was an accomplished Taoist master before his devotion to Zen, I have had the opportunity of being trained in both disciplines, and am therefore in a position to make an informed comparison.

Of the six patriarchs of Zen Buddhism, who were responsible for the foundation of Zen teaching, the first three stayed and taught in Shaolin Monastery; they were Bodhidharma, Hui Ke and Seng Can, and the First Patriarch Temple, Second Patriarch Temple and Third Patriarch Temple built in their honour are found in the extensive Shaolin Monastery complex today. A patriarch is the successor named by the previous patriarch to transmit Zen. There was no significant Taoist influence in Shaolin Monastery, which was regarded as 'the foremost temple beneath heaven' dedicated to Buddhism.

The fourth and fifth patriarchs, Dao Xin and Hong Jen, taught Zen at Dongshan Temple; and the sixth, Hui Neng, taught in Baolin Temple. All of them acknowledged Shaolin Monastery as the mother monastery, and they often returned there to pay their respects. Dongshan and Baolin are typical Buddhist temples where Taoist influence was unknown, and there was no record of Zen in China before the arrival of Bodhidharma.

There was no seventh patriarch because the sixth Patriarch did not appoint a single successor; there were instead many successors, because he asked his disciples to spread his teaching.

A Zen monk is very different from a Taoist priest. He is a strict vegetarian, is celibate and shaves his head as a symbol of having left the mundane life for spiritual cultivation. A Taoist priest is permitted to eat meat and drink wine, marry and keep his hair in a typical Taoist bun, although some Taoists do voluntarily lead a vegetarian and celibate life. Some monks, rightly or wrongly, say that Taoist priests are not ready to give up everything, not even their hair, for the sake of spiritual fulfilment. However, you do not need to become a monk to practise Zen; as in the Shaolin arts of Kung Fu and Chi Kung, if you train conscientiously and diligently, you can become a master without becoming a monk.

While the supreme aim of Zen and Taoism is the same – attaining ultimate reality – their fundamental meditation techniques are different. Taoist mediation makes extensive use of visualization, whereas Zen meditation avoids it and focuses on the void. According to the Zen teaching on meditation, which will be explained in more detail later, although visualization can lead to very high spiritual levels, it does not lead directly to the highest, ultimate reality. But since many Taoists aim not at the realization of ultimate reality or, in Taoist terms, unity with the Cosmos, but at becoming immortals or even just at longevity in this life, meditation using visualization serves their purposes very well.

Probably the most important reason why Zen Buddhism is Buddhism, and not Taoism in Buddhist dress, as some scholars want us to believe, is that all the fundamental teachings of Zen Buddhism, right from the time it first developed in China, are found in the form of Buddhism taught by the Buddha himself. Basic Zen concepts, such as reality being manifested in transcendental or phenomenal dimensions, the rise of thoughts as the cause of delusion, the transmigration of beings in the six realms of phenomenal existence, the role of Bodhisattvas in universal salvation and meditation as the essential way to enlightenment, are basic Mahayana teachings. They are also found in sacred Theravada scriptures today, although most Theravadins may not emphasize them. Zen simply differs from other Buddhist schools in its approach: it seeks to attain enlightenment directly through meditation.

The aim of Zen, the highest of the Shaolin arts, is to experience cosmic reality beyond the phenomena or appearances perceived in ordinary consciousness. This chapter has provided the philosophical understanding necessary for achieving better results more quickly. The practical methods of meditation to achieve the aims of Zen are explained in the next. These methods, which represent the apex of Shaolin Kung Fu training, are the legacy of the greatest of the masters.

16

THE SHAOLIN WAY TO ENLIGHTENMENT

(Methods of Meditation for Spiritual Development)

❖ *The basic doctrine of Zen is to realize ultimate reality, which is tranquil and void. The fundamental way to achieve this is to attain a state where no thoughts abide.*

Attaining a Focused Mind

The highest attainment in the training of Shaolin Kung Fu is spiritual fulfilment. Because of linguistic, cultural and historical differences, teachers of different religions have described their highest spiritual fulfilment in different terms, although they all refer to the same achievement.[1] In the Shaolin tradition, it is known as Zen, and sometimes as *nirvana, bodhi*, or Buddhahood. In English, it is translated as 'enlightenment'.

Zen or enlightenment is the majestic, sublime experience of cosmic reality in its transcendental dimension, where all dualism has disappeared, where the enlightened being is emancipated from the illusory prison of the physical body and becomes the infinite, eternal universe as he or she realizes that the personal mind is in reality the Universal Mind. The essential path to enlightenment is meditation.

The kind of meditation practised in the Shaolin tradition is the one taught by Bodhidharma. It is known as Patriarch Zen, and emphasizes focusing on the void. However, for those with little or no meditation experience, or without any training in Shaolin Kung Fu or Shaolin Chi Kung, it is not easy to focus on the void. It is therefore advisable for them to start with Tathagata Zen, which is the kind of meditation taught by the Buddha himself, and which aims to attain a focused mind.

Tathagata is a Sanskrit term meaning 'suchness', ie cosmic reality without conditions, and it is how the Buddha often referred to himself after he had attained enlightenment, indicating that an enlightened being is in reality the Cosmos as he or she has transcended the illusory boundary of the physical body to which ordinary people confine themselves because of the limitation of their senses. *Tathagata* is *ju lai* in classical Chinese and *ru lai* in modern Romanized Chinese; Tathagata Zen is *ru lai chan*.

The following is a famous meditation technique in Tathagata Zen. It is known as *anapanasati*, and was originally taught by the Buddha himself, and described in the *Satipatthana Sutra* (*Scripture on the Foundation of Mindfulness*).

Sit comfortably in a single or double lotus position in a secluded place where you will not be disturbed throughout the training session. Support your buttocks with a firm pad or pillow if needed. Place your palms on your knees in what is known as the Lohan poise – *figure 16.1 (a)*. This poise will help to keep your spine straight, which is a very important factor in meditation training. When you have become used to sitting comfortably upright, you can progress to placing one palm on your legs in front of you, and the other on it with the thumbs touching slightly – *figure 16.1 (b)*. This is known as the Buddha poise.

Single Lotus Lohan poise

Double Lotus Buddha poise

Fig 16.1 The lotus positions

Sitting in a simple cross-legged position or upright on a chair may be suitable for meditation with a lesser aim, such as for relaxation, stress management, chi training or even developing psychic powers. But for the supreme aim of spiritual fulfilment, you must sit in either the single or the double lotus position. If you legs are too stiff to do so, you need to practise leg stretching exercises to loosen them.

Your body must be upright but relaxed. If your back slumps, you are likely to cause an energy blockage at that spot, which will result in pain or discomfort. Your head must be slightly tilted forward so that if you look ahead, your eyes rest on an extension of your nose level. If you tilt your head backwards, which you might unconsciously do after meditating for some time, the rush of chi up the spine, which may occur in those who have consistently trained for some time, may enter your head at a vital point called *nao-hu* ('house of the brain'), and this may cause deviations such as giddiness, nervousness, pain and hallucination. If your head is tilted forwards slightly forming a smooth curve, the rising chi will flow round your head in a pleasant, beneficial manner. You can, if you wish, place the tip of your tongue against your upper gum; this is helpful for those who are familiar with this position, but might be distracting to others. Your eyes can be gently closed or half-closed, focusing at the tip of your nose.

When you are correctly and comfortably seated, clear your mind of all thoughts. Then gently focus on your breathing. You need not consciously regulate you breath, but just be gently aware of it. Silently count your breath as you breathe out. Count from one to 10, then repeat the counting in sets of 10. In other words, silently count 'one' as you breathe out the first time, count 'two' the second time, until you reach 10, then count 'one' again as you breathe out the eleventh time, 'two' the twelfth time, and so on.

If you miss or lose count, it does not matter; just continue from the first number (between one and 10) that comes to mind. If you find yourself counting to 15, for example, it means you have lost concentration or awareness; continue the next count as 'six'.

If you can perform Abdominal Breathing, you may use it in place of spontaneous breathing, and proceed the same way. Complete the meditation practice by rubbing your palms, warming your eyes with your palms as you open your eyes, loosen your body, then walk about briskly.

This technique of counting breaths is a very effective way of achieving a focused mind. Practise daily for about three months before proceeding to the next stage of *anapanasati*.

Meditation to Train Awareness

After training the mind to be well focused, the next stage is to develop sharp awareness. Use the same method as in counting breaths, except that now, instead of counting you *follow* the breath. You can start your meditation by first counting your breaths a few times, or you can proceed straight to following the breath.

When you breathe in, spontaneously or regulated as part of Abdominal Breathing, be gently aware that you breathe in. When you breathe out, be gently aware that your breathe out. If you are occasionally hesitant, or pause in your breathing, or breathe more quickly than usual, be aware that you are hesitant, pause or breathe more quickly. If your awareness wanders, as often happens, bring it back gently but immediately without fuss or question, and resume your practice.

Later, when you have developed a keen sense of awareness, you can progress to a deeper level of training. As you breathe in, follow your whole in-breath from its entry into your nostril right to where it settles in your lungs, abdomen or other parts of your body. Similarly, as you breathe out, follow your whole out-breath from where it starts its journey right through your body to its exit from your mouth or nose.

In our school, Shaolin Wahnam, we believe in quality rather than quantity in training. We recommend only five minutes of counting or following the breath. If you can successfully count or follow your breath with full awareness for a total of three minutes in your five-minute meditation, you would have done well. It is certainly better than sitting in a meditation position for half an hour, with hardly a minute of full awareness and 29 minutes of myriad thoughts arising. As you progress you can gradually increase the length of each meditation session. But irrespective of whether you meditate for five minutes or 50, your counting or following of the breath must be done gently; any forced concentration is likely to result in deviation.

If you practise the above meditation daily for six months, you will be amazed at the benefits you will get. Not only will your mind be focused and your awareness sharp and fresh, but you will also attain clarity of thought and inner peace. If you practise daily for six years, you will obtain benefits that you may not have dreamed of before. However, if you feel uncomfortable, giddy, nauseous, nervous or frightened, or if you develop a headache or hallucinations, your practise is wrong. Stop and consult a master immediately for remedial action. On the other hand, if you practise for years and do not experience the benefits mentioned above, you should review your training with reference to the Three Requirements for Attainment explained in Chapter 5.

Investigating Cosmic Reality

Buddhism is exceedingly rich in meditation methods, but all of them can be divided into two main groups: *samadha* or tranquil meditation and *vipassyana* or insight meditation. *Samadha* meditation is aimed at taming the mind to attain tranquility, while *vipassyana* meditation is employed to expand the mind, to investigate the true nature of reality.

Anapanasati, the method described in the last section, is a form of *samadha* meditation. When the mind is focused, it can then be employed to investigate ultimate reality in *vipassyana* meditation. There are many ways to approach cosmic investigation. One effective way is to look straight into the mind and ask, while in deep meditation, what that mind is, or where it is located. Another Zen question you can investigate in your *vipassyana* or insight meditation is whether you and your mind are the same. Do not jump from question to question; you need only one question, which if properly asked will lead you to a Zen awakening when you can answer all the other questions, but you must ask the one question as if your whole life depended on its answer.

You may reason and speculate, but you will never get the answer you seek by any intellectual means, because it must be directly experienced. Using the simple analogy mentioned in the previous chapter, the answer to the question of what a mango tastes like cannot be obtained by reasoning and speculation, but only by directly experiencing it. If you persist, over many years or even lifetimes, *prajna* or transcendental wisdom will blossom, and the answer will be right in front of your mind's eye.

Asking awakened people how they know they have the right answer to a Zen question is like asking someone eating a mango how he or she knows what the taste of a mango is. If the teacher asks a seemingly simple question like 'Have you taken a meal?', they may give a seemingly illogical reply like 'That donkey is swimming in the lake'. Yet both they and the teacher find the answer meaningful. Such Zen encounters in the past are now recorded as *gong-ans*, or *koans* in Japanese.

While it is not impossible to achieve awakening from practising insight meditation on one's own, it is obviously a tremendous advantage to train under a master. But if a student, or even the instructor, does not even know what cosmic reality is, or what insight he or she expects to get, but merely calls sitting in a lotus position *vipassyana* meditation because it is fashionable to do so, it is hardly surprising that such a student gains little or no result.

The approach to enlightenment through tranquil and insight meditation, where the mind is trained to be focused and then employed to investigate ultimate reality, is known as Tathagata Zen. This is also the approach employed by most schools of Buddhism, although the types of question they use as a catalyst for their cosmic investigation is different. Theravada Buddhists, for example, frequently derive their questions from the doctrine of dependent origination, investigating such topics as what causes birth and death, what the physical body is made of, and why karma is perpetuated. Mahayana Buddhists often derive their questions from aspects of cosmic reality, investigating topics like what conditions phenomena, what dharmas or subatomic particles are, and what lies beyond mind.

The Zen of Bodhidharma and Hui Neng

Patriarch Zen, or *zu shi chan*, is the form of Zen taught by the first Patriarch and explained in some detail by the sixth Patriarch. Zen was first transmitted by the Buddha to Mahakasyapa, who was the first patriarch of the Indian tradition and who transmitted Zen to the second patriarch, and so on until Bodhidharma, the 28th Indian patriarch. When Bodhidharma brought Zen from India to China, he was regarded by the Chinese and subsequent Zen practitioners of the world as the first Patriarch of the Chinese tradition.

It will normally take a very long time to achieve enlightenment, usually over many reincarnations. In Theravada Buddhism, followers improve their karma by cultivating moral purity so that, hopefully, they will one day be born as monks, to devote all their time to attaining *nirvana*. In Mahayana Buddhism, followers may take upon themselves the great compassionate Bodhisattva's task, vowing to come back to phenomenal worlds again and again to help others. In a way, Zen Buddhism is a reaction against this long journey towards enlightenment; it seeks to attain it here and now, and accomplishes this aim by experiencing ultimate reality directly through meditation. In Zen terms this is pointing directly at the mind and attaining enlightenment in an instant.

Why and how this can be done is explained by the sixth Patriarch Hui Neng in his *Tan Jing* or *Platform Sutra*. Hui Neng is regarded as the Chinese Buddha, and his *Platform Sutra*, together with the *Heart Sutra*, the *Diamond Sutra* and the *Lankavatara Sutra*, constitutes the most important text in Zen Buddhism. The *Platform Sutra* is very clear in its presentation, but those not familiar with concise Buddhist terms may find it difficult to understand. See if you can make sense of the following very important passage, which contains the gist of Zen Buddhism.

> Non-thought constitutes the basic doctrine, non-characteristics constitutes the basic body, and non-abiding constitutes the basic foundation. What is non-characteristics? Non-characteristics is to be in the midst of characteristics yet free from them. Non-thought is to be in the midst of thoughts yet free from thoughts. Non-abiding is the original nature of man. Thought after thought arises, yet they do not abide. Past thoughts, present thoughts, future thoughts – thought after thought is connected, without breaking off, without end. If a thought is broken off, the spiritual body is free from the physical body.[2]

The meaning is as follows. The basic doctrine of Zen is to realize ultimate reality (described in Zen jargon above as non-thought), which is tranquil and void (described as non-characteristics). The fundamental way to achieve this is to attain a state where no thoughts abide (because the illusory external world is a creation of mind).

What is meant by saying that ultimate reality is tranquil and void? It means that when you are awakened or enlightened, you will realize that ultimately there is no dualism, ie there is no differentiation between you and anything else, although ordinary people observing you will see you as a separate person sitting in meditation and all other objects as different entities.

Reality can manifest in two dimensions: the same reality that manifests as the phenomenal world to ordinary people, is transcendental to the enlightened. When an enlightened being does not abide with any thoughts that arise, ultimate reality (described as original nature) is manifested. Countless thoughts may arise but if they are not attached to the being, he or she remains in a state of enlightenment.

The thoughts of ordinary people are continuously connected, from the past to the present to the future; there is not an instant when they are without thoughts. If you can break of this train of continuous thoughts just for an instant, then at that instant you become a buddha, as you liberate your illusory personal mind from your illusory physical body and attain the realization that you are in reality the Universal Mind (described as the spiritual body).

If you understand the above explanation, you will understand why Dogen Eihei (1200–1253), the great Japanese master who founded Soto Zen in Japan, said that when you attain the meditation of no-mind, you are not practising to become a buddha; *you* are a buddha. This reminds us of Hui Neng's famous statement:

When an ordinary person is enlightened he becomes a buddha; when a buddha is unenlightened be becomes an ordinary person.

Soto Zen and Rinzai Zen, or *cao dong chan* and *lin ji chan* in Chinese, are the two most popular schools of Zen in the world today, and both generally employ Patriarch Zen. While Soto Zen emphasizes the meditation of no-mind, Rinzai Zen makes extensive use of *koans* (or seemingly illogical Zen stories) in their spiritual cultivation. Various schools have been practised in Shaolin Monastery, but the most important throughout Shaolin history has been *cao dong chan* or Soto Zen.

The following method of meditation to attain the state of no-mind is so bafflingly simple that people often wonder whether it works. It is the highest meditation taught in the Shaolin tradition. It is the method taught by the greatest of Zen masters, the sixth Patriarch Hui Neng and the first Patriarch Bodhidharma. It can actually be described in one short sentence: go into deep meditation in a lotus position and keep your mind free from all thoughts.

But when you practise this method, unless you have had previous meditation training, or training in Shaolin Kung Fu and Shaolin Chi Kung, you will find it one of the most difficult tasks you have ever tried. For many people, it is helpful to start with counting or following the breath. Only when you have tamed your mind, should you attempt to expand to *mo* mind, which actually means all mind.

Zen seeks to attain enlightenment in an instant, but you must remember that this instant normally takes many years of diligent, conscientious training to achieve. If you are ready, you will first have an awakening, which will be the most beautiful, joyful and amazing experience you will ever have. Your whole perspective towards life and the universe will change after this spiritual experience. You will love all beings, and have no fear of anything, not even death, because you will experience the evidence of your own immortality in this spiritual awakening. You will accept the teachings of the Enlightened Ones not because they are enlightened but because of your own direct experience of their truth.

The awakening is an inspiring confirmation that your path towards enlightenment is correct. The journey from awakening to enlightenment is still long, but you will know it is worth taking. You must also remember that meditation training to achieve a spiritual awakening is the third step, not the first, in the cultivation of enlightenment. The first and second are avoiding all evil and doing good. If you neglect these earlier steps, it is unlikely that you will make much progress in your meditation. This is not moralizing but a universal truth, which you can perceive when you are awakened. If you acquire psychic powers, which will normally happen as you progress in meditation, but use them for selfish or evil purposes, you will inevitably ruin yourself, and end up leading a miserable life or even developing mental problems, as is evident from the stories of some psychics without strong spiritual foundation.

Shaolin Kung Fu for Spiritual Development

You may ask, 'If Zen training or meditation is the path to enlightenment, why bother to practise Shaolin Kung Fu or Shaolin Chi Kung for spiritual fulfilment?' The answer is that if you are not ready, you will achieve little, even if you meditate for years. Shaolin Kung Fu and Shaolin Chi Kung are excellent ways of preparing yourself. Sometimes, even without formal Zen practice, a disciple training in Shaolin Kung Fu or Chi Kung may achieve a high degree of spiritual development, because Zen or meditation is already incorporated in the other two Shaolin arts.

You will achieve the full benefits of meditation training only if you are physically, emotionally, mentally and spiritually fit. If you are sick, emotionally disturbed, mentally dull or spiritually unsettled, you are unlikely to make such progress, and you may sometimes suffer unwanted side-effects. Indeed, it was in order to make the Shaolin monks physically, emotionally, mentally and spiritually fit for the demanding discipline of meditation practice that Bodhidharma introduced the Eighteen Lohan Hands and the Sinew Metamorphosis, which later developed into Shaolin Kung Fu and Shaolin Chi Kung.

The holistic training of Shaolin Kung Fu with Chi Kung makes one physically fit, emotionally stable and mentally fresh: if one is not physically fit, one can hardly fight; if one is not emotionally stable, one cannot apply one's combat skills; if one is not mentally fresh, one cannot make split-second decisions. In the past, when fighting was commonplace, the lack of any one of these qualities might mean the difference between life and death. Fights to the death are fortunately very rare today, but these invaluable qualities, produced by a training system that has been acknowledged as 'the best beneath heaven', can be used to promote spiritual cultivation.

Moreover, a Shaolin Kung Fu disciple is generally spiritually stronger than most other people. This is because one's spirit is directly related to one's state of physical health and energy level. Essence, energy and spirit, or *jing*, chi and *shen*, are closely related: if a our essence is weak (which is manifested as poor health), we will lack energy; if we lack energy, our spirit will be infirm. Some symptoms of a person whose spirit is infirm include being afraid of the dark, nervous of the future, easily frightened by slight movements, and fearful of ghosts. A person who is weak spiritually can be knowledgeable in religious matters, but is usually slow in spiritual cultivation.

Different Attainments for Different Needs

Shaolin Kung Fu, therefore, leads to the greatest achievement any person can ever attain, ie the highest spiritual fulfilment. Nevertheless, some people may not be ready for or interested in this highest spiritual training. In Buddhism there are methods to meet the various needs and aspirations of different people, which can be divided into the following three generalized levels:

1 Live healthily and happily to a ripe old age.
2 Go to heaven in the next life.
3 Attain the greatest, highest achievement, described variously as attaining enlightenment, achieving Buddhahood, returning to God, union with Allah, unity with the Cosmos, becoming one with Brahman, seeing ultimate reality, or finding the Absolute Truth.

Shaolin Kung Fu, in conjunction with the teaching of Buddhism, can help us to achieve any or all of these aims. Practising Shaolin Kung Fu daily can ensure that we live healthily to a ripe old age. And to ensure that our healthy, long life is also happy, we practise the basic teaching of the Buddha, namely avoiding evil, doing good and purifying the mind.

Numerous writers have been impressed by the fact that in many Asian countries where the dominant religion is Buddhism, the people are always cheerful and courteous. It is obvious, even to the most sceptical, that those who do not cheat or steal, but are always kind and helpful to others irrespective of whether they are kings or paupers, have every reason to be happy. Their feeling of being at peace with themselves and with others is further enhanced if they also spend a few minutes a day meditating.

For those who want to go to heaven in their next life, Buddhism provides the best guarantee. There are good reasons for this claim. While there is only one heaven in most other religions, in Buddhism even in our world system alone, known as the Saha World, there are 22; there are literally countless heavens in countless other world systems in countless galaxies in the known universe where we can go to if we wish and if we qualify – and Buddhism shows the way.

In Buddhism it is comparatively easy to go to heaven. The main qualification is to accumulate good karma by avoiding evil and doing good. A rebirth in heaven is not a reward by the Buddha or any divine being, but the result of karmic effect. All one's thoughts, words and deeds, both good and bad, are imprinted in one's mind, and after the disintegration of the physical body at death, one's mental vibrations will attract appropriate *dharmas* (or subatomic particles and forces) for rebirth at an appropriate place according to the karmic effect of the vibrations.

One's thought at the moment of death has a great influence over one's next rebirth. If, owing to bad karma, one dies a violent death, the impression of pain and fear in one's mind is not likely to give one a good rebirth. On the other hand, if one dies serenely, satisfied that one has led a good life, the feeling of peace and satisfaction in one's consciousness at the very moment of his passing away will probably lead to a rebirth in heaven. Masters who have attained a high level of meditation can not only tell when they will leave this world, but also decide where they want to go in their next. They do so by an intense concentration on the heaven of their choice at the moment of their transmigration.

But going to heaven is not the highest aim in Buddhism. Heavens, like hells and other worlds, are still in the phenomenal realm; they are still creations of mind. The supreme aim of Buddhism is Buddhahood or enlightenment, where the enlightened one goes nowhere but breaks down all illusory boundaries and differentiation, and transcends the phenomenal realm. One realizes that one is the infinite, eternal Cosmos, or the omnipresent, omniscient ultimate reality, which is described by some as God.

Zen, the highest level to which Shaolin Kung Fu leads, aims to achieve this sublime, unsurpassed attainment here and now. It is, of course, a formidable task, but if you are determined, and have fulfilled the prerequisites of avoiding evil and doing good, you too can succeed by purifying your mind using the methods taught by the Enlightened Ones themselves as explained in this book. The result is inexplicable, but as a poor analogy may be described as eternal, infinite bliss. If you can comprehend the magnitude of the opportunity facing you, you will appreciate why great princes and kings, like the Buddha, Bodhidharma, King Subhakarasinha of Orissa, Padmasambhava, Mahindra and King Tran-Thai-Ton of Vietnam, renounced their luxurious palace lives to seek and help others to seek the greatest, highest attainment.

NOTES

Chapter 1

[1] For a comprehensive study of Taijiquan, see my book *The Complete Book of Taijiquan*, Element Books, Shaftesbury, 1996.

Chapter 2

[1] Cited in Xi Yun Tai, *History of Chinese Martial Arts*, People's Sports Publications, Beijing, 1985, p.122. In Chinese.

Chapter 3

[1] For a comprehensive study of Chi Kung, see my book, *The Art of Chi Kung*, Element Books, Shaftesbury, 1993.

[2] The Romanized spelling of this word is *qi*, but since *chi* is generally used in English, this is the spelling used here. The other two terms, *jing* and *shen* are spelt in the Romanized way.

Chapter 14

[1] For a comprehensive study of Chi Kung, see my book *The Art of Chi Kung*, Element Books, Shaftesbury, 1993.

Chapter 15

[1] Quoted in Dr Graham Phillips, *The Missing Universe*, Penguin Books Australia, 1994, p.70.

[2] Cited in Pierre Rousseau, *The Limits of Science*, translated by John Newell, Scientific Book Club, London, 1968, pp.132–3.

Chapter 16

[1] See Chapter 21 of my book, *The Art of Chi Kung*, Element Books, Shaftesbury, 1993.

[2] Hui Neng, *Platform Sutra*. In Chinese, translated by the author.

FURTHER READING

In English

Alan Watts, *The Way of Zen*, Vintage Books, New York. 1989. First pub. 1957.

Daisetzu Teitaro Suzuki, *An Introduction to Zen Buddhism*, Grove Press, New York. 1991. First pub. 1964.

Dalai Lama Tenzin Gyatso, Tr. by Donald Lopez Jr., Wisdom Publications, London. 1985.

David Scott and Tony Doubleday, *The Elements of Zen*, Element, Shaftesbury. 1993. First pub. 1992.

Dr W F Jayasuriya, *The Psychology and Philosophy of Buddhism*, Buddhist Missionary Society, Kuala Lumpur. 1988. First pub. 1963.

Dwight Goddard (ed), *A Buddhist Bible*, Beacon Press, Boston. 1994. First pub. 1938.

General Tao Hanzhang, *Sun Tzu's Art of War*, Tr. from the Chinese by Yuan Shibing. Eastern Dragon Books, Kuala Lumpur. 1991.

James MacRitchie, *Chi Kung: Cultivating Personal Energy*, Element, Shaftesbury. 1993.

John Blofeld, *Taoism: the Quest for Immortality*, Unwin Hyman, London. 1989. First pub. 1979.

John Snelling, *The Elements of Buddhism*, Element, Shaftesbury. 1994. First pub. 1990.

Louis Frederic, *Buddhism: Flammarion Iconographic Guides*, Flammarion. New York. 1995.

Martin Palmer, *The Elements of Taoism*, Element, Shaftesbury. 1991.

Narada Maha Thera, *A Manual of Abhidhamma: an Outline of Buddhist Philosophy*, Buddhist Missionary Society, Kuala Lumpur. 1979. First pub. 1976.

Paravahera Vajirasana Mahathera, *Buddhist Meditation in Theory and Practice*, Buddhist Missionary Society, Kuala Lumpur. 1975. First pub. 1962.

Sangharakshita, *A Survey of Buddhism: its Doctrines and Methods Through the Ages*, Windhorse Publications, Glasgow. 1993. First pub. 1957.

Shunryu Suzuki, *Zen Mind. Beginner's Mind*, Weatherhill, New York. 33rd printing 1994. First pub. 1970.

Thich Nhat Hanh, *Zen Keys: a Guide to Zen Practice*, Doubleday, New York. 1995. First pub. in French 1973; first pub. in English 1974.

Wong Kiew Kit, *Introduction to Shaolin Kungfu*, Paul Crompton, London. 1994. First pub. 1981. (Please note: in this book the spelling used is 'Kungfu')

Wong Kiew Kit, *The Art of Chi Kung*, Element, Shaftesbury. 1993.

Wong Kiew Kit, *The Complete Book of Tai Chi Chuan*, Element, Shaftesbury. 1996.

Xing Yan and others, *Shaolin Kungfu: Treasure of the Chinese Nation, the Best of Chinese Wushu* (Bilingual), China Pictorial Publishing House, Beijing. 1985. (Please note: in this book the spelling used is 'Kungfu')

Ying Zi and others, *Shaolin Kung Fu*, Kingsway International Publications, Hong Kong. 1981.

In Chinese

A rich collection of books in the Chinese language is available. The selection of the following books for further reading is based on their high value and authenticity.

General

Editorial Committee, *Martial Artists and Martial Arts*, Shanghai Educational Publications, Shanghai. 1985.

Editorial Committee of Wulin Magazine, *Collection of Traditional Techniques for Force Training*, Science and General Publications, Guangzhou. 1989.

Fang Jin Hui and others (ed), *Encyclopedia of Chinese Martial Arts*, Anwei People's Publications, Anwei. 1987.

Li Zong Wu, *Chinese Military Strategies*, Pictorial Books, Hong Kong. Undated.

Lu Guang Ming, *Pocket Encyclopedia of Martial Arts*, Hubei Educational Publications, Hubei. 1986.

Qui Pi Xiang, *Introduction to Martial Arts*, Shanghai Educational Publications, Shanghai. 1985.

Wang Jian Dong, *Military Strategies of Sun Tzu*, Zhi Yang Publications, Taiwan. 1994.

History

Xi Yun Tai, *History of Chinese Martial Arts*, People's Physical Education Publications, Beijing. 1985.

Xiongtian Fengzhi (Japanese). Tr. by Lu Yan and Yan Feng Ze, *Discussion on the History of Chinese Martial Arts*, Sichuan Science and Technology Publications, Chendu. 1984.

Shaolin

Cheng Zong Dou, *Principles of Shaolin Staffs and Spears*, (A reproduction of ancient text), Chen Xiang Ji Books, Hong Kong. Undated.

Chunwoji Juren, *Secrets of Shaolin Kungfu*, Taiping Books, Hong Kong. 1983.

Li Ying Ang, *Pictorial Explanation on Shaolin Principles*, (A reproduction of ancient text), Unicorn Press. 1968.

Liang Yi Chuan (ed), *Fist Techniques of Songshan Shaolin Kungfu*, Shandong Education Publications. 1982.

Liu Zhi Xue (ed), *Collections of Shaolin Material*, Literary and Cultural Publications, Beijing. 1982.

Venerable Te Qian and others (ed), *The Genuine Seventy Two Arts of Shaolin*, Beijing Physical Education Publications, Beijing. 1990.

Venerable Te Qian, *The True Transmission of Shaolin Kungfu*, Beijing Physical Education Publications, Beijing. 1990.

Wang Hong Jun, *Folklore Concerning the Shaolin Monastery*, Henan People's Publications, Chengdu. 1981.

Wang Hong Jun and others (ed), *Shaolin Poetry*, Henan People's Publications, Chengdu. 1985.

Wu Jia Ming (ed), *Secret Techniques of Shaolin Force Training*, Fujian Science and Technology Publications, Fujian. 1990.

Zhao Bao Jun, *Shaolin Monastery*, Shanghai People's Publishing House, Shanghai. 1982.

Xue Hou, *Precious and Genuine Records of the Shaolin Monastery*, Guangdong Science and Technology Publications, Guangzhou. 1983.

Zhao Shi, *Legends of Southern Shaolin*, Mantingfang Publishing House, Taipei. 1993.

Zhang Guo Chen and Lu Jiang Shui (ed), *Selection of Shaolin Poetry*, Tourism Publications, Beijing. 1985.

Zen and Taoism

Huang Zhao and others (ed), *History of Taoist Thoughts*, Hunan Teachers' Training University Press. 1991.

Song Ze Lai (ed), *Zen Sutras in Modern Language*, Baiseng Publishing House, Hong Kong. Undated.

Venerable Dong Chu, *History of Thoughts on the Heart Sutra*, Dong Chu Publications, Taipei. 1990.

Venerable Hui Guang, *Gateway to the Study of Zen*, Dafeng Cultural Publications, Taipei. Undated.

Venerable Sheng Yan, *Experience of Zen*, Dong Chu Publications, Taipei. 1993.

Zhu Yue Li, *Questions on Taoism*, Cultural Publications, Beijing. 1989.

Useful Addresses

Malaysia

Grandmaster Wong Kiew Kit
81 Taman Intan B/5
08000 Sungai Petani
Kedah, Malaysia
Tel: (60-4) 422-2353
Fax: (60-4) 422-7812
URL:
http://shaolin-wahnam.tripod.com
E-mail: shaolin@pd.jaring.my

Master Cheong Huat Seng
22 Taman Mutiara
08000 Sungai Petani
Kedah, Malaysia
Tel: (60-4) 421-0634

Master Goh Kok Hin
86 Jalan Sungai Emas
08500 Kota Kuala Muda
Kedah, Malaysia
Tel: (60-4) 437-4301

Master Chim Chin Sin
42 Taman Permai
08100 Bedong
Kedah, Malaysia
Tel: (60-4) 458-1729
Mobile Phone: (60) 012-552-6297

Master Morgan A/L Govindasamy
3086 Lorong 21, Taman Ria
08000 Sungai Petani
Kedah, Malaysia
Tel: (60-4) 441-4198

Master Ng Kowi Beng
20, Lorong Murni 33
Taman Desa Murni Sungai Dua
13800 Butterworth
Pulau Pinang, Malaysia
Tel: (60-4) 356-3069
Fax: (60-4) 484-4617
E-mail : kowibeng@tm.net.my

Master Yong Peng Wah
Shaolin Wahnam Chi Kung and
Kung Fu
181 Taman Kota Jaya
34700 Simpang, Taiping
Perak, Malaysia
Tel: (60-5) 847-1431

Australia

Mr. George Howes
33 Old Ferry Rd, Banora Point
NSW 2486, Australia
Tel: 00-61-7-55245751

Austria

Sylvester Lohninger
Maitreya Institute
Blättertal 9
A-2770 Gutenstein
Tel: 0043-2634-7417
Fax: 0043-2634-74174
E-mail: sequoyah@nextra

Belgium

Dr. Daniel Widjaja
Steenweg op Brussel 125
1780 Wemmel, Belgium
Tel: 00-32-2-4602977
Mobile Phone: 00-32-474-984739
Fax: 00-32-2-4602987
E-mail: dan_widjaja@hotmail.com
daniel.widjaja@worldonline.be

Canada

Miss Emiko Hsuen
67 Churchill Avenue, North York,
Ontario M2N 1Y8, Canada
Tel: 1-416-250-1812
Fax: 1 - 416- 221-5264
E-mail: emiko@attcanada.ca

Dr. Kay Lie
E-mail: kayl@interlog.com

Mrs. Jean Lie
Toronto, Ontario
Tel/Fax: (416) 979-0238
E-mail: kayl@interlog.com

Columbia & Costa Rica

Master Roberto Lamberti
E-mail: robertolamberti@libero.it

England

Mr. Christopher Roy Leigh Jones
9a Beach Street, Lytham, Lancashire
FY8 5NS, United Kingdom
Tel: 0044-1253-736278
E-mail: barbara.rawlinson@virgin.net

Mr. Dan Hartwright
Rumpus Cottege, Church Place
Pulborough, West Sussex
RH20 1AF, UK
Tel: 0044-7816-111007
E-mail: dhartwright@hotmail.com
cosmosuk@hotmail.com

Germany

Grandmaster Kai Uwe Jettkandt
Ostendstr. 79
60314 Frankfurt, Germany
Tel: 49-69-90431678
E-mail: Kaijet@t-online.de

Holland

Dr. Oetti Kwee Liang Hoo
Tel: 31-10-5316416

Ireland

Miss Joan Brown
Mullin, Scatazlin, Castleisland
County Kerry, Ireland
Tel: 353-66-7147545
Mobile Phone: 353-87-6668374
E-mail: djbrowne@gofree.indigo.ie

Italy

Master Roberto Lamberti
Hotel Punta Est Via Aurelia, 1
17024 Finale Ligure (SV), Italy
Tel: ++39019600611
Mobile Phone: ++393393580663
E-mail: robertolamberti@libero.it

Master Attilio Podestà
Via Aurelia 1
17024 Finale Ligure (Savona), Italy
Tel/Fax: +39 019 600 611
E-mail: attiliopodesta@libero.it
or
Hotel Punta Est Via Aurelia 1
17024 Finale Ligure (Savona), Italy
E-mail: info@puntaest.com
Web-site: www.puntaest.com

Dr. Riccardo Puleo
via don Gnocchi, 28
20148 Milano, Italy
Tel: 0039-02-4078250
E-mail:
rpuleo@efficient-finance.com

Lithuania

Mr. Arunas Krisiunas
Sauletekio al.53-9
2040 Vilnius, Lithuania
Tel: +3702-700-237
Mobile Phone: +370-9887353
E-mail: induva@iti.lt

Panama

Mr. RaulA. LopezR.
16 "B" St.
Panama City, Republic of Panama
Mailing Address: PO Box 1433
Panama 9A-1433 Panama
E-mail: raullopez@cwpanama.net
taikO@hotmail.com

Portugal

Master Riccardo Salvatore
Shaolin Wahnam Chi Kung
Praca Afranio Peixoto 2, 1°Dto
1000-009 Lisboa, Portugal
Tel: 351-218478713
Fax: 351-218421174
E-mail:
chikung.shaolin.wahnam@clix.pt

Scotland

Mr. Darryl Collett
c/o 19A London Street, Edinburgh
EH3 6LY, United Kingdom
Mobile Phone: 0790-454-7538
E-mail: CollDod@aol.com

Spain

Master Laura Fernández
C/ Madre Antonia de París
2 esc. izq. 4° A
28027 Madrid, Spain
Tel: 34-91-6386270
E-mail: salabriefing@iberia.es

Javier Galve
Tai Chi Chuan and Chi Kung
Instructor of the Shaolin Wahnam
Institute
C/Guadarrama 3-2°A
28011 Madrid, Spain
Tel: 34-91-4640578
Mobile Phone: 34-656669790
E-mail: shaolin@inicia.es

Master Adalia Iglesias
calle Cometa, n° 3, atico
08002 Barcelona, Spain
Tel: 0034-93-3104956
E-mail: adalia@xenoid.com

Master José Díaz Marqués
C/. del Teatro, 13
41927 Mairena del Aljarafe
Sevilla, Spain
Tel: + 34-954-183-917
Mobile Phone: 34-656-756214
Fax: + 34-955-609-354
E-mail:
transpersonal@infotelmultimedia.es

Dr. Inaki Rivero Urdiain
Aguirre Miramon, 6 – 4° dch.
20002 San Sebastian, Spain
Tel: + 34-943-360213
Mobile Phone: 34-656-756214
E-mail: psiconet@euskalnet.net
Web-site:
www.euskalnet.net/psicosalud

Master Douglas Wiesenthal
C/ Almirante Cadarso 26, P-14
46005 Valencia, Spain
Tel/Fax: +34 96-320-8433
E-mail: dwiesenthal@yahoo.com

Master Trini
Ms Trinidad Parreno Agullo
Capitan Antonio Mena-103
Postcode.3201 Elche
Alicante, Spain
Tel: 966665094
Mobile phone: 609441770
E-mail: trinipar@wanadoo.es

South Africa

Grandmaster Leslie James Reed
312 Garensville, 285 Beach Road
Sea Point, Cape Town
8000 South Africa
Tel/Fax: 0927-21-4391373
E-mail: itswasa@mweb.co.za

Switzerland

Master Andrew Barnett
Bildweg 34
7250 Klosters, Switzerland
Tel/Fax: +41-81-422-5235
Mobile Phone: +41-79-610-3781
E-mail: andrew.barnett@bluewin.ch

USA

Mr. Anthony Korahais
546 W147th Street, Apt. 2-DR
New York, NY, 10031
Tel: 917-270-4310, 212-854-0201
E-mail: anthony@korahais.com
anthony@arch.columbia.edu

Mr. Eugene Siterman
299 Carroll St.
Brooklyn, NY, 11231
Tel: 718-855-5785
E-mail: qipaco@hotmail.com
cosmosnyc@hotmail.com

INDEX